Scandinavian Recipes Yr.

Can Cook in An Hour

Quick and Effortless Ways to Prepare Scandinavian Dishes

BY Yannick Alcorn

Copyright Warnings

Table of Contents

Introduction

Fall in love with the same recipes again and again with this collection of 30 deliciously easy dishes. In addition to being nutritious and delicious, the dishes in this collection can be prepared in under an hour.

With *"Scandinavian Recipes You Can Cook in An Hour,"* quick and effortless meals don't have to be boring. Get ready to cook classics like Danish buttermilk soup and chokladsnittar that will become regulars in your weekly meal rotation and fulfill your appetites.

Cut down on time spent in the kitchen without sacrificing an ounce of taste. All of the recipes come together quickly with common ingredients and simple preparation methods anyone can master. Enjoy the process of cooking these appetizing meals that never take long from prep to plate.

You'll find yourself turning to these recipes over and over when you need a healthy, hassle-free and utterly delicious meal on the table quickly. So, say goodbye to long ingredient lists and fussy techniques; these fuss-free recipes will have you falling in love meal after meal.

AAAAAAAAAAAAAAAAAAAAAAA

1. Polar Bear Cocktail

The sky is not the only thing that is blue!!! This Swedish cocktail is all shades of blueeee!!

Preparation Time: 04 minutes

Cook Time: nil

Serve: 1

List of Ingredients:

- 1 ounce of Blue Curaçao
- 2 ounces of Absolut vodka
- 1 ounce of Sprite

AAAAAAAAAAAAAAAAAAAAAAA

Methods:

A. Begin by pouring the desired amount of vodka and Blue Curaçao into a glass.
B. Thoroughly mix the contents to ensure even distribution of flavors.
C. Top off the mixture with Sprite, adding a refreshing fizz to the cocktail.
D. Introduce ice cubes to the glass, chilling the drink and enhancing its crispness.
E. Give the cocktail a good stir, marrying the ingredients and maintaining a consistent taste.
F. Take a moment to savor and enjoy the Polar Bear Cocktail.

Cooking Notes:

- Alcohol Proportions: Adjust the quantities of vodka and Blue Curaçao based on personal preference and desired alcohol content. Start with equal parts and modify as needed.

- Mixing Technique: When mixing the vodka and Blue Curaçao, use a gentle stirring motion to avoid excessive dilution or loss of carbonation from the Sprite.

- Glass Choice: Opt for a clear glass to showcase the cocktail's vibrant blue color, enhancing its visual appeal.

- Sprite Variation: Experiment with Sprite variations like diet or flavored Sprite to introduce unique flavor dimensions.

- Ice Considerations: Use quality ice cubes to prevent rapid melting and dilution of the cocktail. You can also consider using ice made from filtered water to ensure purity.

- Stirring: Stirring the cocktail after adding ice helps to maintain an even temperature and consistent taste throughout the drinking experience.

- Garnish: Elevate the presentation by garnishing with a twist of lemon peel or a maraschino cherry. The contrasting colors provide a delightful visual contrast.

- Glassware: While not essential, serving the cocktail in a chilled glass can enhance the overall experience.

- Serving: This cocktail is best enjoyed on a warm day or as a refreshing evening treat. Consider pairing it with light appetizers or hors d'oeuvres.

- Responsible Consumption: Remember to enjoy alcoholic beverages responsibly and be mindful of your alcohol tolerance. Always drink in moderation.

2. Blueberry Oatmeal Porridge

Make your breakfast a delightful one with this nutritious and tasteful meal!

Preparation Time: 03 minutes

Cook Time: 15 minutes

Serve: 1

List of Ingredients:

- 1 cup of blueberry jam

For the oatmeal

- 1 pinch of salt
- 1 mashed ripe banana
- 1 pinch of cinnamon
- 1 cup of soy milk
- 1 tbsp of hemp seeds
- 8 tbsp of oats

For toppings

- 1 tsp of butter (almond)
- 1 pinch of bee pollen
- 1 tsp of chopped walnuts

AAAAAAAAAAAAAAAAAAAAAAAA

Methods:

A. Start by bringing the soy milk to a boil in a pan.

B. Add a pinch of salt and the oats to the boiling milk.

C. Allow the mixture to cook for about 3 minutes, stirring occasionally, until it thickens to your desired consistency.

D. Turn off the heat and introduce the mashed ripe banana, a pinch of cinnamon, and the hemp seeds to the oatmeal. Stir well to combine all the flavors.

E. Serve the creamy oatmeal in bowls.

F. Enhance the dish's flavor and presentation by garnishing with a dollop of blueberry jam on top.

G. For added richness, stir in a teaspoon of almond butter into each bowl.

H. Sprinkle a pinch of bee pollen over each serving to add a unique texture and a touch of sweetness.

I. Finally, top the oatmeal with a teaspoon of chopped walnuts for a satisfying crunch.

Cooking Notes:

- Blueberry Jam: Opt for a high-quality blueberry jam with a balanced sweetness to complement the oatmeal's flavors.

- Oatmeal Consistency: Adjust the cooking time according to your preference for oatmeal thickness. Some prefer it thicker, while others like a slightly looser texture.

- Banana Mashing: Make sure the banana is ripe and well-mashed for a natural sweetness that blends seamlessly with the oatmeal.

- Soy Milk Variation: Feel free to use your preferred milk or milk substitute, such as almond milk or oat milk, in place of soy milk.

- Hemp Seeds: Hemp seeds add a nutty flavor and a boost of nutrition. You can substitute with chia seeds or flax seeds if desired.

- Sweetness Adjustments: Depending on the sweetness of the banana and jam, you can adjust the amount to suit your taste. Taste the oatmeal before adding extra sweeteners.

- Cooking Technique: Stirring occasionally while cooking the oatmeal prevents it from sticking to the bottom of the pan and ensures even cooking.

- Cinnamon Sprinkling: Cinnamon adds warmth and depth to the oatmeal. Adjust the amount to your liking and sprinkle it evenly to incorporate its flavor throughout.

- Ripe Banana: The riper the banana, the sweeter it is. Ripe bananas also mash more easily, creating a smoother texture.

- Texture Variation: For more texture, consider leaving some banana chunks in the oatmeal for bursts of sweetness.

- Nut Butter Alternatives: Experiment with different nut butters, such as peanut butter or cashew butter, for varied flavors.

- Allergen Information: Be mindful of allergens when serving bee pollen, nuts, or nut butter, especially if you're serving to a group of people.

- Seed Swap: If you don't have hemp seeds, you can replace them with other seeds like sunflower seeds or pumpkin seeds.

- Quick Toppings: If you're short on time, you can use pre-made blueberry jam and nut butter.

- Layering Technique: When layering the toppings, consider starting with the almond butter as a base to hold the other toppings in place.

- Protein Boost: To further increase the protein content, you can sprinkle a spoonful of chia seeds on top.

- Nutritional Value: This oatmeal is rich in fiber, healthy fats, and nutrients from the seeds, nuts, and banana.

- Gluten-Free Option: Ensure that your oats are certified gluten-free if you're following a gluten-free diet.

- Child-Friendly: This oatmeal is a great way to introduce healthy ingredients to children while still appealing to their taste preferences.
- Texture and Flavor Contrast: The combination of creamy oatmeal, crunchy nuts, and chewy blueberry jam creates a delightful mouthfeel.
- Ingredient Prep: Having your ingredients measured, chopped, and prepared in advance can streamline the cooking process.
- Hydration: Consider having a glass of water or a cup of herbal tea alongside your oatmeal to stay hydrated.
- Custom Bowl: Serve the oatmeal in your favorite bowl to make the experience more enjoyable.
- Serving Size: Adjust the quantities based on how many servings you need. This recipe can easily be scaled up or down.
- Food Photography: If you're into food photography, this oatmeal's vibrant colors and layers make it a visually appealing subject.
- Mindful Eating: Take a moment to appreciate the flavors, textures, and colors as you enjoy each bite of your Blueberry Oatmeal Porridge.
- Topping Variations: Customize the toppings with other options like sliced fresh berries, chopped almonds, or a drizzle of honey.
- Bee Pollen: Bee pollen not only adds texture but also provides potential health benefits. However, avoid it if you have allergies to pollen or bee products.
- Almond Butter: Almond butter enriches the oatmeal with a creamy texture and nutty taste. You can choose other nut butters as well.
- Presentation: To create an Instagram-worthy presentation, carefully layer the toppings and jam to create a visually appealing dish.
- Serving: Enjoy this Blueberry Oatmeal Porridge as a wholesome breakfast or a nourishing snack to keep you energized throughout the day.

3. Nordic Honey Punch

Incorporate honey, herbs, and milk together to get this sweet-sour Scandinavian Punch!!

Preparation Time: 06 minutes

Cook Time: nil

Serve: 1

List of Ingredients:

- 2 ounces of lemon (Juice)
- 2 ounces of Campari
- 6 ounces of milk
- 2 ounces of syrup (honey)
- 6 ounces of Aquavit
- 2 ounces of Vermouth

AAAAAAAAAAAAAAAAAAAAAA

Methods:

A. Begin by mixing Campari, syrup, and vermouth in a shaker.
B. Shake the mixture thoroughly to ensure proper blending of flavors.
C. In a separate pan, bring milk to a gentle boil.
D. Remove the pan from heat and stir in aquavit and freshly squeezed lemon juice.
E. Strain the milk mixture into the shaker containing the initial mixture.
F. Shake the combined mixture again to achieve a harmonious blend.
G. Finally, strain the punch into a glass, ensuring any ice or solid ingredients are strained out.
H. Take a moment to savor and enjoy the Nordic Honey Punch.

Cooking Notes:

- Campari Choice: Campari is a bitter liqueur with a distinct flavor. Adjust the quantity based on your preference for bitterness and overall taste.

- Syrup Variation: The choice of syrup can impact the punch's sweetness. Adjust the syrup quantity to achieve the desired level of sweetness.

- Vermouth Selection: Use dry vermouth for a less sweet profile or sweet vermouth for a richer and slightly sweeter taste.

- Boiling Milk: When boiling milk, be cautious to avoid scalding or burning. Stirring gently while heating can help prevent sticking to the pan.

- Aquavit: Aquavit is a traditional Scandinavian spirit with herbal and spice flavors. Ensure it's of good quality for the best taste.

- Lemon Juice: Freshly squeezed lemon juice adds a tangy brightness to the punch. Adjust the amount based on your preference.

- Straining: Straining the milk mixture before combining with the initial mix helps remove any curdled bits, resulting in a smoother texture.

- Glass Choice: Choose glassware that showcases the punch's color and allows space for ice or garnishes.

- Garnishes: Consider garnishing the punch with a twist of lemon peel, a slice of citrus, or a fresh herb like mint.

- Serving: Nordic Honey Punch can be enjoyed as an aperitif or a refreshing cocktail. It pairs well with appetizers or light snacks.

- Temperature: If desired, you can serve this punch over ice for a chilled experience.

- Presentation: A visually appealing presentation can enhance the overall enjoyment. Clean glassware, proper garnishes, and a well-prepared drink can elevate the experience.

- Responsible Consumption: As with any alcoholic beverage, remember to enjoy in moderation and be mindful of alcohol tolerance.

4. Swedish Rose Spritz

Refreshingly amazing for a sunny summer day!

Preparation Time: 05 minutes

Cook Time: nil

Serve: 1

List of Ingredients:

- 4 ounces of dry rose wine
- 1 ounce of lemon seltzer water
- 2 ounces of elderflower liqueur

AAAAAAAAAAAAAAAAAAAAA

Methods:

A. Fill a glass with ice cubes to create a refreshing base for your drink.

B. Pour in the rose wine, allowing its floral notes to combine harmoniously with the upcoming ingredients.

C. Enhance the flavors by adding the desired amount of liqueur into the glass, giving your spritz a unique twist.

D. Gently stir the mixture to ensure that the wine and liqueur blend seamlessly.

E. Introduce a spritz of excitement by adding a dash of lemon seltzer water, creating a delightful fizz and a hint of citrus.

F. Stir the concoction once again to evenly distribute the seltzer water and infuse your drink with effervescence.

G. Complete your drink with an elegant touch by garnishing it with a thin slice of lemon. This adds a visual appeal and a zesty aroma.

Cooking Notes:

- Glass Choice: Opt for a wine glass or a highball glass, both of which work well for this spritz.

- Ice Matters: The ice cubes not only chill the drink but also dilute it slightly as they melt, mellowing the flavors.

- Wine Selection: Choose a rose wine with the desired level of sweetness and aroma. The wine forms the foundation of your spritz, so selecting a quality one is key.

- Liqueur Options: Experiment with various liqueurs like elderflower, raspberry, or even a subtle herbal one to add complexity to your drink.

- Seltzer Water: Adjust the amount of lemon seltzer water to achieve the desired level of effervescence and tartness.

- Garnish Variation: Aside from lemon slices, you can also use rose petals or other edible flowers for a touch of elegance.

- Presentation: A well-garnished drink is not only visually appealing but also heightens the overall drinking experience.

- Sipping Experience: This Swedish Rose Spritz is best enjoyed slowly, savoring each sip to appreciate the layers of flavors.

- Alcohol-Free Option: For a non-alcoholic version, replace the rose wine and liqueur with a combination of grape juice and flavored sparkling water.

- Customization: Feel free to adjust the quantities of each ingredient to match your taste preferences.

5. Chokladsnittar

Don't let the long names stress you or put you off. These crispy chocolate cookie slices are not only classic but delicious beyond imagination!!

And they are very easy to prepare too!!!

Preparation Time: 10 minutes

Cook Time: 10 minutes

Serve: 20 pieces

List of Ingredients:

- 3 tbsp of pearl sugar
- 1 cup of flour
- 1 tsp of baking powder
- 100g of butter
- 1 tsp of vanilla sugar
- 4 tbsp of powdered sugar
- 2 tbsp of cocoa
- 1 small egg

AAAAAAAAAAAAAAAAAAAAAAA

Methods:

A. Begin by preheating your oven to 402 degrees Fahrenheit (205 degrees Celsius), ensuring it's ready for baking.

B. In a mixing bowl, combine the pearl sugar and softened butter, blending them until you achieve a smooth mixture.

C. Incorporate the vanilla sugar, cocoa powder, all-purpose flour, and baking powder into the bowl. Continue mixing until the ingredients form a cohesive and well-mixed dough.

D. Work the dough until it reaches a fine texture, ensuring all the ingredients are evenly distributed and the dough is ready for shaping.

E. On a clean surface, roll out the dough to a thickness of approximately 2 centimeters, forming 4 to 5 lengths of dough.

F. Using a knife or cookie cutter, cut the dough lengths into the desired shapes, as depicted in the image provided.

G. Place the shaped dough pieces on baking sheets lined with parchment paper, ensuring they have enough space between them for even baking.

H. To enhance the appearance and flavor, brush the tops of the dough shapes with beaten egg, which will give them a beautiful golden sheen when baked.

I. Add a delicate sprinkle of powdered sugar over the brushed dough shapes, contributing a touch of sweetness and visual appeal.

J. Slide the baking sheets into the preheated oven and bake the Chokladsnittar for approximately 10 minutes. Keep an eye on them to avoid overbaking; they should be slightly golden around the edges.

K. Once baked, carefully remove the Chokladsnittar from the oven and allow them to cool on a wire rack or a flat surface.

L. Once the Chokladsnittar have cooled down completely, they are ready to be savored and enjoyed as a delightful treat.

Cooking Notes:

- Pearl Sugar: Pearl sugar adds texture and sweetness to the Chokladsnittar. You can find it in specialty baking stores or online.

- Dough Consistency: Ensure that the dough is well-mixed and uniform in texture to prevent uneven baking.

- Shaping and Cutting: The dough can be shaped and cut into various sizes and designs, allowing for creative customization.

- Egg Wash: Brushing the dough with beaten egg adds shine and color to the finished cookies.

- Powdered Sugar: A light dusting of powdered sugar after brushing with egg enhances the appearance and flavor.

- Baking Time: Baking times may vary based on your oven, so monitor the Chokladsnittar closely to avoid burning.

- Storage: Store the cooled Chokladsnittar in an airtight container to maintain their freshness.

- Serving: These cookies are ideal for serving with coffee, tea, or as a sweet snack.

6. Danish Buttermilk Soup

This traditional Scandinavian (most especially of Danish roots) buttermilk soup is not just delicious, but it is your best bet on a hot summer day!!!

Preparation Time: 10 minutes

Cook Time: nil

Serve: 3

List of Ingredients:

- 2 cups of plain yogurt
- 1 pinch of vanilla extract
- 2 cups of buttermilk
- 1 tsp of sugar
- 2 egg yolks
- 1 tsp of lemon juice
- 1 tbsp of cane sugar

AAAAAAAAAAAAAAAAAAAAAAA

Methods:

A. Begin by combining the sugar, vanilla extract, and egg yolk in a bowl. Mix these ingredients together until they become light and fluffy, resulting in a creamy base for your soup.

B. Gradually introduce the yogurt into the mixture. This step adds tanginess and a velvety texture, enhancing the overall flavor profile.

C. Pour in the buttermilk and a splash of lemon juice. Thoroughly mix these components to achieve a harmonious blend that balances the sweetness and tanginess of the soup.

D. Once the mixture is well-mixed, place it in the refrigerator to chill. Allowing the soup to chill enhances the flavors and provides a refreshing temperature when it's time to serve.

E. When you're ready to serve, retrieve the chilled buttermilk soup from the refrigerator. This step ensures that the soup is perfectly cool and inviting.

F. As a final touch, garnish the soup with halved strawberries. The strawberries not only add visual appeal but also contribute a burst of fruity flavor.

Cooking Notes:

- Egg Yolk Mixture: Mixing the sugar, vanilla extract, and egg yolk until light and fluffy helps incorporate air and create a smooth, sweet base for the soup.

- Yogurt Addition: Adding yogurt enriches the soup's texture and introduces a delightful tangy note.

- Buttermilk and Lemon Juice: The combination of buttermilk and lemon juice provides a balanced tanginess and a refreshing quality to the soup.

- Chilling Time: Allowing the soup to chill allows the flavors to meld and ensures that it's served at the optimal temperature.

- Garnish: Halved strawberries not only enhance the presentation but also add a fruity element that complements the creamy soup.

- Serving Vessel: Consider serving the Danish Buttermilk Soup in small bowls or cups, allowing the garnish to shine.

- Variations: You can experiment with different fruit garnishes like blueberries, raspberries, or even a sprinkle of cinnamon.

- Texture Preference: If you prefer a smoother consistency, you can blend the soup using a blender or immersion blender before chilling.

- Customization: Adjust the amount of sugar and lemon juice to achieve your preferred level of sweetness and tanginess.

- Serving Occasion: This soup can be served as a light dessert, a refreshing starter, or even a palate cleanser between courses.

7. Lingonberry Sauce

Something new and tasty that you can put together in less than an hour!!!

Preparation Time: 07 minutes

Cook Time: 12 minutes

Serve: 6

List of Ingredients:

- 8 tbsp of sugar
- 4 tbsp of water
- 2 cups of lingonberries

AAAAAAAAAAAAAAAAAAAAAAA

Methods:

A. Begin by placing the lingonberries in a pan along with a bit of water. This will create a base for your sauce.

B. Cook the berries in the pan for about 5 minutes. This gentle cooking process will start breaking down the berries and releasing their natural flavors.

C. After the berries have cooked, introduce the sugar to the pan. Stir the mixture continuously for approximately 4 minutes to ensure that the sugar completely dissolves into the sauce.

D. Let the mixture simmer for about 7 more minutes. This simmering time allows the sauce to thicken and develop a luscious consistency.

E. Once the sauce has achieved the desired thickness, remove it from the heat. The lingonberry sauce is now ready to be enjoyed.

F. Serve the lingonberry sauce warm, perhaps drizzled over a stack of fluffy pancakes for a delicious and tangy topping.

Cooking Notes:

- Berries: Lingonberries are a tart and flavorful berry commonly used in Scandinavian cuisine. If using frozen berries, allow them to thaw before cooking.

- Water: Adding a bit of water to the pan prevents the berries from sticking and burning as they start to cook.

- Sugar Dissolution: Stirring the sugar into the berry mixture and allowing it to dissolve ensures that the sauce has a consistent sweetness throughout.

- Simmering Time: Allowing the sauce to simmer further thickens it and intensifies the flavors.

- Consistency Check: You can test the sauce's consistency by placing a small amount on a cold plate. If it thickens as it cools, it's ready.

- Serving Temperature: Lingonberry sauce can be served warm or at room temperature, depending on your preference.

- Versatility: This sauce isn't limited to just pancakes; it can also be served alongside meats, poultry, or other dishes for a burst of tartness.

- Storage: Leftover lingonberry sauce can be stored in an airtight container in the refrigerator for several days.

- Enhancements: For added depth of flavor, consider incorporating a touch of orange zest or a splash of orange juice.

8. Daiquiri

With Aquavit, this daiquiri recipe tastes different from the rest!!!

Preparation Time: 04 minutes

Cook Time: nil

Serve: 1

List of Ingredients:

- 2 ounces of Aquavit
- 1 ounce of sugar syrup
- 1 dash of lime juice

AAAAAAAAAAAAAAAAAAAAAA

Methods:

A. Begin by assembling the ingredients you'll need: You'll require 2 ounces of Aquavit, 1 ounce of sugar syrup, and a dash of lime juice.

B. In a glass filled with ice, combine the three ingredients listed. This combination will create the base of your Daiquiri.

C. Stir the mixture well, ensuring that all the ingredients are thoroughly combined and chilled.

D. Your Daiquiri is now ready to be enjoyed. Savor the unique flavors and refreshing qualities of this classic cocktail.

Cooking Notes:

- Aquavit: Aquavit is a Scandinavian spirit known for its distinctive flavor profile, often featuring caraway and other botanicals.
- Sugar Syrup: Sugar syrup adds sweetness and balances the flavors of the cocktail. You can adjust the amount based on your preference for sweetness.
- Lime Juice: The dash of lime juice provides a tangy and citrusy element that brightens the cocktail.
- Glass Choice: Traditionally, Daiquiris are served in a cocktail glass or a tumbler with ice.
- Ice: Using ice helps chill the cocktail and dilute it slightly as the ice melts.

- Stirring: Stirring the cocktail ensures that the ingredients are mixed evenly and that the flavors meld together.
- Garnish: For added visual appeal, you can garnish the cocktail with a twist of lime peel or a lime wheel.
- Aquavit Selection: Choose a high-quality Aquavit that you enjoy. Different brands and types may have varying flavor profiles, so consider exploring different options.
- Sugar Syrup Options: You can use simple syrup, which is equal parts water and sugar dissolved together, as a sweetener. Alternatively, you can use flavored syrups for a unique twist.
- Lime Juice Freshness: Freshly squeezed lime juice adds a vibrant and zesty flavor. Make sure your lime juice is freshly squeezed for the best taste.
- Cocktail Mixing: If you have a cocktail shaker, you can shake the ingredients with ice for a more intense chill and aeration.
- Ice Quality: Use quality ice to prevent excess dilution and to maintain the flavor integrity of the cocktail.
- Glassware: While a cocktail glass is traditional, you can also use a rocks glass or a highball glass, depending on your preference.
- Chilling Method: If you prefer your cocktail without ice, you can stir the ingredients in a mixing glass and strain them into a chilled glass.
- Proportions: Adjust the proportions of Aquavit, sugar syrup, and lime juice to create a balance that suits your taste buds.
- Flavor Experimentation: Aquavit has a range of flavors, so feel free to experiment with different styles to find your preferred combination.
- Cocktail Etiquette: Stirring a cocktail with ice chills and dilutes it while also blending the ingredients. This method is used for spirit-forward cocktails like the Daiquiri.
- Sip and Savor: Take small sips of your Aquavit Daiquiri to appreciate the evolving flavors as the ice melts and the cocktail warms slightly.

- Daiquiri History: The Daiquiri is a classic cocktail with a rich history, originating in Cuba. Exploring its history can add an interesting context to your drink.

- Temperature: A well-chilled cocktail glass enhances the drinking experience. Consider chilling the glass in the freezer for a few minutes before assembling the cocktail.

- Balance: The balance of sweet, sour, and spirit is key to a great cocktail. Adjust the ratios to achieve the desired balance for your taste preferences.

- Cocktail Ritual: Preparing and enjoying cocktails can be a relaxing and creative experience. Take your time to craft the perfect Aquavit Daiquiri.

- Responsible Drinking: Enjoy your cocktail responsibly and be mindful of alcohol content. If you're unsure about the effects, pace yourself and know your limits.

- Aquavit Education: If you're new to Aquavit, take a moment to learn about its production process, flavor profile, and cultural significance.

- Culinary Pairing: Consider pairing your Aquavit Daiquiri with Scandinavian-inspired dishes to create a cohesive dining experience.

- Variations: While the classic Daiquiri uses rum, this variation with Aquavit offers a unique twist. You can experiment with other spirits or flavors as well.

- Serving Occasion: Daiquiris are versatile and suitable for various occasions, from casual gatherings to more formal events.

- Customization: Adjust the proportions of the ingredients to suit your taste preferences.

9. Finnish Lohikeitto

This Scandinavian delicacy is not just easy to prepare, but it is also delicious and flavorful!!!

Preparation Time: 07 minutes

Cook Time: 15 minutes

Serve: 2

List of Ingredients:

- 2 tbsp of butter
- 3 cups of chunked skinless salmon (boneless)
- 1 tbsp of pepper
- 1 tsp of allspice
- 2 cups of fish stock
- 3 cups of diced russet potatoes
- 1 medium sliced carrot
- 2 medium sliced leeks
- 8 tbsp of heavy cream
- 1 pinch of salt
- 2 handfuls of chopped dill

AAAAAAAAAAAAAAAAAAAAAAA

Methods:

A. Begin by sautéing the leeks in melted butter, allowing their flavor to infuse the base of the soup.

B. Cook-fry the leeks for about 7 minutes, giving them time to soften and develop a slightly caramelized aroma.

C. Add the stock to the pot, creating a flavorful liquid foundation for your Finnish Lohikeitto.

D. Introduce the dill, carrots, and potatoes into the pot, adding layers of taste and texture to the soup.

E. Toss in the salmon, cream, a pinch of pepper, and a dash of salt, enhancing the richness and creaminess of the soup. You can also add your preferred spices at this stage.

F. Allow the mixture to cook until the salmon is done and the flavors have melded together beautifully.

G. Once the Finnish Lohikeitto is cooked to perfection, it's ready to be served and enjoyed as a hearty and comforting dish.

Cooking Notes:

- Leeks: Sautéing the leeks in butter at the beginning imparts a savory and aromatic base to the soup.

- Cook-Frying: Cooking the leeks for 7 minutes helps soften them and develop their flavors without browning them too much.

- Stock: Adding stock, often fish or vegetable-based, forms the main liquid component of the soup.

- Dill: Dill is a crucial herb in Finnish Lohikeitto, contributing a fresh and herbal aroma.

- Carrots and Potatoes: These root vegetables add heartiness and substance to the soup.

- Broth Variation: You can choose between fish or vegetable broth for the base. Fish broth intensifies the seafood flavor, while vegetable broth adds a lighter note.

- Salmon Skin: Leaving the skin on the salmon during cooking can add extra flavor and texture to the soup. Just remember to remove it before serving if you prefer a skinless presentation.

- Cooking Salmon: The salmon should be gently simmered until it's opaque and flakes easily. Overcooking can lead to a dry texture, so keep an eye on it.

- Herb Options: While dill is traditional, you can also experiment with other fresh herbs like chives, tarragon, or parsley to personalize the flavor.

- Cream Alternatives: To lighten the soup, you can replace some or all of the cream with milk or a dairy-free milk substitute.

- Potato Varieties: Use waxy potatoes, like Yukon Gold, for the soup. They hold their shape better during cooking.

- Vegetable Additions: If desired, you can add other vegetables such as peas, corn, or even spinach for added color and nutrients.

- Creamy Consistency: Use an immersion blender to partially blend some of the soup if you prefer a creamier consistency with chunks of vegetables.

- Reheating: When reheating leftover soup, do so gently over low heat to prevent curdling of the cream.

- Meal Complete: Finnish Lohikeitto is a complete meal with protein, vegetables, and dairy. It's both comforting and nourishing.

- Serving Dish: Serve the soup in deep bowls or mugs for a cozy dining experience.

- Bread Pairing: Crusty bread, rye bread, or Finnish-style ruisleipä are traditional accompaniments that complement the soup well.

- Flavor Melding: Allow the soup to rest for a short time after cooking. This helps the flavors meld even more, resulting in a richer taste.

- Frozen Salmon: You can use frozen salmon for convenience. Just thaw it before adding it to the soup.

- Lactose-Free: If you're lactose intolerant, you can replace the cream with a lactose-free alternative, such as almond milk or coconut cream.

- Healthier Version: For a lighter version, you can use a mixture of broth and milk instead of heavy cream.

- Storage: Store any leftover soup in an airtight container in the refrigerator. Reheat gently on the stovetop, stirring occasionally.

- Seasonal Twist: Consider adding seasonal vegetables to the soup to make it even more vibrant and in tune with the time of year.

- Sustainability: Opt for sustainably sourced salmon to make your dish environmentally conscious.

- Cultural Experience: Preparing and enjoying traditional dishes like Finnish Lohikeitto offers insight into the food culture of different regions.
- Stock Quality: If you have the time, consider making your own homemade fish or vegetable stock for an even richer base flavor.
- Family Favorite: Finnish Lohikeitto is a wholesome option that can be enjoyed by the whole family. It's a way to introduce different flavors to your loved ones.
- Salmon: Adding salmon pieces, often boneless and skinless, provides a protein-rich element and a signature taste.
- Cream: Cream enriches the soup, lending it a velvety and luxurious texture.
- Spices: Depending on personal preference, you can add a variety of spices like white pepper, nutmeg, or even a pinch of cayenne for a subtle kick.
- Cooking Time: The soup should be cooked until the salmon is fully cooked and flakes easily. Be careful not to overcook the salmon, as it can become dry.
- Serving: Finnish Lohikeitto is often served as a main course, accompanied by crusty bread or crackers.
- Garnish: A sprig of fresh dill or a dollop of sour cream can serve as a lovely garnish.
- Cultural Context: Finnish Lohikeitto is a traditional salmon soup enjoyed in Finland, especially during the colder months.

10. Scandinavian Pop

The tarty taste of Ginger gives this Berry drink a flavorful lift!!

Preparation Time: 04 minutes

Cook Time: nil

Serve: 1

List of Ingredients:

- 1 splash of lemon juice
- 3 ounces of cranberry juice
- 3 ounces of vodka (raspberry flavor)
- 1 dash of ginger ale

AAAAAAAAAAAAAAAAAAAAAAAA

Methods:

A. Begin by mixing the juices and vodka in a shaker filled with ice. This combination forms the flavorful base of your Scandinavian Pop cocktail.

B. Shake the mixture vigorously in the shaker. This step not only blends the ingredients but also chills the cocktail.

C. Strain the shaken mixture into a glass, ensuring that the ice from the shaker is left behind.

D. Add the ginger ale to the strained mixture. The ginger ale adds a refreshing effervescence and a touch of sweetness to the cocktail.

E. Your Scandinavian Pop cocktail is now ready to be enjoyed. Sip and savor the delightful flavors of this fizzy and vibrant drink.

Cooking Notes:

- Juices: The combination of juices, often citrusy and fruity, provides a balanced and refreshing flavor profile to the cocktail.

- Vodka: Vodka is a versatile spirit that adds a neutral base to the cocktail, allowing the other flavors to shine.

- Shaking: Shaking the mixture with ice not only mixes the ingredients but also cools them down quickly.

- Straining: Straining the mixture ensures that only the liquid part of the cocktail is poured into the glass, leaving behind the ice and any potential pulp.

- Ginger Ale: Adding ginger ale gives the cocktail a pleasant fizziness and a hint of ginger flavor.

- Glass Choice: You can serve this cocktail in a highball glass or another glass of your choice.

- Garnish: Consider garnishing the cocktail with a citrus slice or twist, adding a visual and aromatic element.

- Variations: You can experiment with different types of juices and variations of ginger ale for different flavors and textures.

- Alcohol Content: The vodka contributes to the alcoholic content of the cocktail. Adjust the amount of vodka based on your preference for strength.

- Serving Occasion: Scandinavian Pop is a refreshing option for social gatherings, parties, or even as a relaxing drink at home.

- Customization: Feel free to adjust the ratios of juices, vodka, and ginger ale according to your taste.

11. Black Rice and Salmon Salad

This is one Salad recipe that you can never get enough of!!!

Preparation Time: 08 minutes

Cook Time: 15 minutes

Serve: 2

List of Ingredients:

- 1 tbsp of mirin seasoning
- 2 tsp of miso paste
- 1 tsp of grated ginger
- 1 peeled Lebanese cucumber (cut into ribbon shapes)
- 1 sliced green shallot
- 2 sliced radishes
- 1 sliced medium avocado
- 80g of black rice
- 1 tbsp of honey
- 1 tsp of coconut oil
- 1 skinless salmon filet (flakes)

AAAAAAAAAAAAAAAAAAAAAAA

Methods:

A. Start by preheating the oven to 386 degrees Fahrenheit (approximately 197 degrees Celsius).

B. Cook the black rice until it's done. Once cooked, drain the rice and rinse it under cold water to stop the cooking process and cool it down.

C. In a bowl, combine the grated ginger, miso paste, mirin, and honey. This mixture will serve as a flavorful dressing for the salad.

D. Season the salmon with your preferred seasonings. Place the seasoned salmon aside, ready to be cooked.

E. In a pan, heat some oil until it's hot. Carefully fry the salmon in the hot oil. Fry until the salmon is golden and crispy on all sides.

F. Once the salmon is golden, transfer it to a baking pan.

G. Pour the miso mixture over the fried salmon in the baking pan. This flavorful mixture will infuse the salmon with delicious umami and sweetness.

H. Bake the salmon in the preheated oven for about 4 minutes. After baking, set the salmon aside for later use.

I. In a large mixing bowl, combine the cooked black rice, sliced cucumber, chopped shallots, sliced radish, diced avocado, and flaked salmon.

J. Toss the ingredients well to ensure an even distribution of flavors and textures in the salad.

K. Your Black Rice and Salmon Salad is ready to be served. Plate the salad and garnish it with a drizzle of the juice from the baking pan for an extra layer of flavor.

Cooking Notes:

- Black Rice: Black rice has a nutty flavor and chewy texture. Ensure that the rice is properly cooked and cooled before assembling the salad.
- Miso Dressing: The mixture of grated ginger, miso paste, mirin, and honey creates a flavorful and umami-rich dressing that enhances the taste of the salad.
- Salmon Seasoning: Season the salmon according to your taste preference. Common seasonings include salt, pepper, and herbs.
- Frying Salmon: Frying the salmon creates a crispy outer layer while keeping the inside tender. Make sure to cook it until it's golden on all sides.
- Baking Salmon: Baking the salmon briefly after frying helps infuse it with the miso mixture's flavors and ensures it's cooked through.
- Tossing: Tossing the ingredients gently helps distribute the flavors and textures evenly.
- Garnish: Drizzling the salad with the juice from the baking pan adds a finishing touch of flavor and moisture.
- Customization: You can add other vegetables, herbs, or nuts based on your preferences.
- Serving: Serve the salad as a light and nutritious meal on its own or as a side dish.

12. Glogg

This heady Swedish mulled wine is a combination of rich wines, spices, grains, and nuts!

Preparation Time: 07 minutes

Cook Time: 12 minutes

Serve: 4

List of Ingredients:

- 2 cups of red wine (dry)
- 1 orange (juiced)
- 1 lemon (juiced)
- 2 handfuls of raisins
- 1 cinnamon stick
- 2 handfuls of blanched almonds
- 1 tsp of sugar
- 2 tsp of bitters
- 1 grated piece of ginger
- 1 cup of sweet white wine
- 3 cloves
- 3 cardamom pods

AAAAAAAAAAAAAAAAAAAAAAA

Methods:

A. In a pan, combine the dry red wine, freshly squeezed orange juice, and lemon juice. Also, add the peels of the orange and lemon for extra citrus aroma.

B. Toss in the blanched almonds, raisins, and a teaspoon of sugar into the pan with the wine and juices.

C. Place the pan over medium heat and add a grated piece of ginger, cloves, and cardamom pods to infuse the mixture with warm and aromatic flavors.

D. Bring the mixture to a boil and let it gently bubble for about 8 minutes. This will allow the ingredients to meld together and the flavors to intensify.

E. After boiling, reduce the heat to a simmer and continue to cook the mixture for an additional 4 minutes. Simmering will help the flavors further develop while ensuring the alcohol content evaporates slightly.

F. Once the Glogg has simmered and the flavors are well-combined, it's time to serve. Ladle the warm and fragrant Glogg into serving glasses or mugs.

G. For an extra layer of complexity, garnish each serving with a dash of bitters. This will enhance the aromatic profile of the drink.

H. To further elevate the visual and aromatic appeal, add a cinnamon stick and a few cardamom pods as garnish. These spices not only enhance the presentation but also infuse the Glogg with their distinctive flavors.

I. Your Glogg is now ready to enjoy! Sip on this delightful warm drink, savoring the rich blend of spices and the comforting warmth of the wine.

Cooking Notes:

- Choice of Wines: Using a dry red wine as the base and sweet white wine adds a balance of flavors and sweetness to the Glogg. It's essential to choose wines you enjoy drinking since their quality will impact the final taste of the drink.

- Citrus Peels: The peels of the orange and lemon contribute essential oils and citrusy notes to the Glogg. Make sure to use organic fruits or thoroughly wash and scrub the peels before adding them to the mixture.

- Alcohol Evaporation: Simmering the Glogg helps evaporate some of the alcohol content while maintaining the rich flavors of the drink. This makes it suitable for a wider range of preferences.

- Quantity Adjustments: You can adjust the quantity of ingredients to make a larger or smaller batch of Glogg, depending on the number of servings you need.

- Storage: If you have leftover Glogg, you can store it in the refrigerator and gently reheat it before serving. The flavors may continue to meld and intensify over time.

- Variations: While the classic Glogg recipe is wonderful, you can also experiment with your favorite spices, fruits, or sweeteners to create your unique twist on this festive drink.

- Warmth and Comfort: Glogg is not only about the flavors but also the warmth it brings to your senses. Enjoy it by a fireplace or while watching the snowfall for an enhanced experience.

- Serving Vessels: Use heat-resistant glasses or mugs to serve Glogg. Consider preheating them with hot water before pouring in the warm drink.

- Cultural Significance: Glogg has a rich history and cultural significance in Scandinavian countries, particularly during the holiday season. Learning about its traditions can add depth to your enjoyment.

- Aromatherapy: The combination of spices and citrus peels in Glogg creates a delightful aroma. As you sip, take a moment to inhale the fragrant steam for an added sensory experience.

- Appetizer Pairing: Glogg pairs well with traditional Scandinavian holiday treats like ginger cookies, saffron buns, or gingerbread.

- Non-Alcoholic Version: If you prefer a non-alcoholic version, you can make a "glögg light" by using grape juice, apple cider, or cranberry juice as the base.

- Ingredients Quality: High-quality spices, fresh citrus, and good wine contribute to the overall excellence of the Glogg. Invest in fresh and flavorful ingredients for the best results.

- Share and Enjoy: Glogg is a wonderful drink to share with friends and family during festive occasions. The process of making it can be a social activity too.

- Personalization: Make Glogg your own by adjusting the spices, sweetness, and garnishes according to your preferences. Experiment and find your perfect blend.

- A Beverage for All: Glogg can be enjoyed by both those who love wine and those who don't typically drink alcohol, as its flavors and warmth are truly inviting to all.

- Sipping Ritual: Glogg is a drink to savor slowly. Take your time to enjoy the layers of flavors that unfold with each sip.
- Blanched Almonds: Blanching the almonds (briefly immersing them in boiling water and then rinsing with cold water) helps remove the skins, resulting in a smoother texture and nutty flavor in the drink.
- Infusing Spices: Adding spices like ginger, cloves, and cardamom pods enhances the warmth and complexity of the Glogg. These spices are key to creating the characteristic flavors of this traditional Scandinavian drink.
- Boiling and Simmering: Boiling the mixture initially helps the ingredients blend and flavors meld. Simmering afterward ensures the drink doesn't overheat, preserves the alcohol content, and lets the flavors continue to develop.
- Garnishes: Bitters, cardamom pods, and a cinnamon stick provide a visual and aromatic flourish. Bitters can vary in intensity, so start with a small amount and adjust to taste.
- Serving: Glogg is traditionally served warm, especially during the colder months. The spices and warmth make it a perfect cozy drink for gatherings and celebrations.

13. Nordic Summer

Do you want a refreshing and crisp cocktail for your summer mood?! This Scandinavian cocktail got you!!

Preparation Time: 06 minutes

Cook Time: nil

Serve: 1

List of Ingredients:

- 1 ounce of lime juice
- 1 ounce of Aperol
- 2 ounces of Aquavit

AAAAAAAAAAAAAAAAAAAAAA

Methods:

A. In a shaker filled with ice cubes, combine 1 ounce of lime juice, 1 ounce of Aperol, and 2 ounces of Aquavit.
B. Shake the mixture vigorously to ensure all the ingredients are well combined and the drink is thoroughly chilled.
C. Using a strainer, pour the mixed cocktail into a chilled glass.
D. To add a finishing touch, garnish the cocktail with a slice of orange. This will not only enhance the presentation but also complement the flavors of the drink.

Cooking Notes:

- Balancing Flavors: The combination of lime juice, Aperol, and Aquavit creates a refreshing and complex flavor profile. Lime juice adds tanginess, Aperol contributes a hint of bitterness and citrus, while Aquavit brings a unique herbal and spice note.

- Shaking Technique: When shaking the cocktail, the ice cubes help chill and dilute the drink slightly while also creating a frothy texture. Shake the shaker with enthusiasm for about 15-20 seconds to achieve the desired chill and dilution.

- Straining: Straining the cocktail as you pour it into a glass helps keep any ice shards or larger bits of ice out of the final drink. This ensures a smoother and more enjoyable sipping experience.

- Glassware: Choose a glass that suits the style of the cocktail. A classic martini glass or a lowball glass would work well for the Nordic Summer cocktail.

- Garnish: Adding an orange slice as a garnish enhances both the visual appeal and the overall taste of the drink. The citrusy aroma from the garnish can also complement the flavors of the cocktail.

- Serving: This Nordic Summer cocktail is perfect for warm weather gatherings and celebrations. It offers a balanced and intriguing combination of flavors that's sure to be a hit among your guests. Serve alongside appetizers or light summer fare.

- Aquavit Choice: There are different varieties of Aquavit available, each with its unique flavor profile. Choose one that you enjoy and that complements the other ingredients in the cocktail.

- Personalization: Feel free to adjust the ingredient quantities based on your taste preferences. You can experiment with the ratios to find the perfect balance of flavors for your palate.

14. Nordic Snapper

The perfect morning cocktail to help you have an awesome day!!!

Preparation Time: 04 minutes

Cook Time: nil

Serve: 1

List of Ingredients:

- 1 pinch of cayenne pepper
- 1 dash of lemon juice
- 1 pinch of ground black pepper
- 1 handful of olives
- 1 pinch of salt
- 2 ounces of Aquavit
- 2 ounces of tomato juice
- 1 lemon wedge

AAAAAAAAAAAAAAAAAAAAAA

Methods:

A. In a glass filled with ice, combine a pinch of cayenne pepper, a dash of lemon juice, a pinch of ground black pepper, and a pinch of salt.

B. Pour in 2 ounces of Aquavit and 2 ounces of tomato juice to the glass with the spice mixture.

C. Stir the mixture gently to ensure the ingredients are well combined and the flavors are evenly distributed.

D. Garnish the Nordic Snapper cocktail with a lemon wedge and a handful of olives. The lemon wedge adds a fresh citrus aroma, while the olives contribute a savory and briny element to the drink.

Cooking Notes:

- Aquavit Choice: Aquavit is a traditional Scandinavian spirit flavored with various herbs and spices. Choose a high-quality Aquavit that suits your taste preferences and complements the other ingredients in the cocktail.

- Spice Levels: The pinch of cayenne pepper adds a subtle kick of heat to the drink, but you can adjust the amount based on your spice tolerance. Similarly, the ground black pepper adds depth and warmth to the cocktail.

- Tomato Juice: Use a good-quality tomato juice for the base of the cocktail. You can also use a Bloody Mary mix if you prefer a more intense flavor profile.

- Lemon Juice: The dash of lemon juice adds a bright and tangy element to balance the flavors. Freshly squeezed lemon juice is preferred for the best taste.

- Garnish: The garnishes play a crucial role in enhancing the presentation and flavor of the cocktail. The lemon wedge adds visual appeal and a burst of citrus aroma, while the olives offer a savory and slightly salty note.

- Glassware: A highball glass or a classic cocktail glass works well for serving the Nordic Snapper. Choose a glass that showcases the cocktail's color and allows space for garnishes.

- Serving: This cocktail is great for summer gatherings, brunches, or whenever you're in the mood for a refreshing and slightly spicy drink. It pairs well with a variety of appetizers and light bites.

- Customization: As with any cocktail, feel free to adjust the ingredient quantities to suit your taste preferences. If you enjoy a stronger drink, you can increase the amount of Aquavit, and if you prefer a milder flavor, you can decrease the spices.

- Ice: Using ice in the glass not only chills the cocktail but also helps to dilute the drink slightly as the ice melts, which can mellow the flavors and make the cocktail more enjoyable.

15. Mint Julep

With just three ingredients, you can prepare this cocktail in the twinkle of an eye!!!

Preparation Time: 03 minutes

Cook Time: nil

Serve: 1

List of Ingredients:

- 200 ml of Aquavit
- 4 tbsp of caster sugar
- 1 bunch of mint leaves (muddled)

AAAAAAAAAAAAAAAAAAAAAA

Methods:

A. Place sugar and muddled mint leaves into a glass, combining sweetness and aromatic mint flavors.
B. Add ice cubes to the glass, creating a chilled base for the drink.
C. Pour in the aquavit, a traditional Scandinavian spirit with herbal and spice notes that complements the mint.
D. Stir the mixture well to dissolve the sugar and ensure the flavors are evenly distributed throughout the cocktail.

Cooking Notes:

- Choice of Aquavit: The choice of aquavit plays a significant role in the final flavor of the Mint Julep. Select an aquavit with a profile that complements the mint and adds depth to the drink.
- Muddled Mint: Muddling the mint leaves releases their essential oils and aroma, infusing the cocktail with refreshing mintiness. Use a muddler or the back of a spoon to gently crush the mint leaves against the sugar.
- Sugar Dissolution: By placing sugar at the bottom of the glass and muddling it with the mint, you create a base that helps dissolve the sugar more effectively when combined with the liquid components.

- Ice: The addition of ice not only chills the cocktail but also dilutes it slightly as the ice melts. This dilution can mellow the flavors and create a more balanced drink.

- Stirring: Stirring the cocktail is essential to combine all the ingredients thoroughly and ensure the sugar and mint are evenly distributed.

- Glassware: A traditional Mint Julep is often served in a metal or glass julep cup, but you can use any suitable glass. The shape of the glass can influence the drink's presentation and how well the mint aroma is captured.

- Garnish: A mint sprig is a classic garnish for a Mint Julep. Slap the mint sprig gently between your palms before placing it in the drink to release its aroma.

- Serving: The Mint Julep is a classic cocktail often associated with warm weather and outdoor events. It's a refreshing choice for social gatherings, particularly those with a Southern or traditional theme.

- Experimentation: While the Mint Julep traditionally includes aquavit, you can also experiment with other spirits like bourbon or gin for a different take on this beloved cocktail.

- Adjusting Sweetness: The amount of sugar can be adjusted based on your preference for sweetness. You can start with the recommended amount and adjust it as needed after tasting the cocktail.

- Refreshing Element: Mint Juleps are known for their refreshing qualities, making them a delightful option for sipping on hot days or at cocktail parties.

16. Meatball Sauce

Made with delicious, creamy, and rich ingredients, this sauce is flavorful and exciting!!

Preparation Time: 08 minutes

Cook Time: 15 minutes

Serve: 3

List of Ingredients:

- 2 tbsp of panko bread crumbs
- 2 tbsp of chopped onion
- 1 pinch of salt
- 1 pinch of pepper
- 1 cup of beef broth
- 1 tsp of Dijon mustard
- 2 cups of ground beef
- 1 pinch of grated nutmeg
- 1 pinch of ground allspice
- 1 handful of chopped parsley
- 1 pinch of powder garlic
- 1 medium egg
- 2 tbsp of olive oil
- 1 tbsp of flour
- 3 tbsp of butter
- 1 tsp of Worcestershire sauce
- 8 tbsp of heavy cream

AAAAAAAAAAAAAAAAAAAAAAA

Methods:

A. In a bowl, combine chopped onion, diced bell pepper, salt, minced garlic, ground beef, chopped parsley, panko breadcrumbs, nutmeg, an egg, and allspice. Mix the ingredients until well blended.

B. Shape portions of the mixture into meatballs, rolling them between your palms to create uniform shapes.

C. Heat a mixture of butter and oil in a pan. Add the meatballs and cook-fry them, turning to ensure even browning on all sides. This develops a flavorful crust.

D. Continue cooking the meatballs until they are cooked through and browned on all sides. Transfer them to a plate.

E. In the same pan, add flour and stir until it's browned. This forms the base for the sauce and helps thicken it.

F. Pour in heavy cream and broth, followed by mustard, ground black pepper, salt, and your choice of sauce. Stir well and cook until the sauce thickens.

G. Return the meatballs to the pan and cook for an additional 2 minutes, allowing them to absorb the flavors of the sauce.

H. Serve the meatballs with the prepared sauce.

Cooking Notes:

- Meatball Mixture: Combining various ingredients like onion, bell pepper, garlic, spices, and breadcrumbs adds depth and flavor to the meatballs.

- Uniform Meatballs: Shaping uniform meatballs ensures even cooking. Rolling them between your palms helps create consistent sizes.

- Cook-Frying Method: Cook-frying the meatballs in a mixture of butter and oil imparts flavor and a desirable caramelized exterior. Avoid overcrowding the pan for even cooking.

- Cooking Vessels: Choose a pan that allows enough space for the meatballs to cook and brown without overcrowding. A wide skillet or sauté pan works well.

- Meat Options: While the recipe mentions ground beef, you can use a combination of meats like pork and beef for added flavor complexity. Ground chicken or turkey can also be used for a lighter version.

- Portion Control: If you're aiming for a consistent size, you can use a cookie scoop or ice cream scoop to portion out the meat mixture before shaping into meatballs.

- Browning Tips: When cook-frying the meatballs, avoid constantly flipping them. Allow them to develop a nice crust on one side before turning to the next. This helps prevent sticking.

- Sauce Consistency: Adjust the amount of flour used for the roux to control the thickness of the sauce. More flour results in a thicker sauce, while less flour creates a lighter sauce.

- Sauce Flavoring: Experiment with adding a splash of Worcestershire sauce or a dash of hot sauce to the sauce for an extra layer of flavor.

- Make-Ahead: You can prepare the meat mixture and shape the meatballs in advance, refrigerating them until you're ready to cook and serve.

- Temperature Check: Use a meat thermometer to ensure the meatballs are cooked to the desired internal temperature (usually 160-165°F or 71-74°C).

- Cream Alternative: If you prefer a lighter sauce, you can replace part or all of the heavy cream with milk or a dairy-free alternative.

- Freezing: Meatballs freeze well. Once cooked, you can freeze them in an airtight container. Thaw and reheat them in the sauce when you're ready to serve.

- Cultural Interpretation: Different cuisines have their own versions of meatballs with unique flavor profiles. Exploring these variations can lead to delightful culinary discoveries.

- Texture Balance: The combination of the crispy exterior of the meatballs and the velvety sauce creates a satisfying contrast in textures.

- Time Management: To save time, you can start preparing the sauce while the meatballs are cooking. This ensures that everything is ready to be combined at the end.
- Sauce Consistency: If your sauce becomes too thick, you can thin it out with a bit of extra broth or cream until it reaches your desired consistency.
- Family-Friendly: Meatballs in creamy sauce are often loved by both kids and adults. It's a versatile dish that can be appreciated by a wide range of palates.
- Leftovers: Leftover meatballs and sauce can be used as filling for sandwiches, wraps, or even as a topping for pizza.
- Savory Side: This dish can be served alongside vegetables, sautéed greens, or a simple salad for a complete and balanced meal.
- Sauce Pairing: Consider serving the meatballs and sauce with a side of lingonberry jam or cranberry sauce for a sweet-tart contrast.
- Texture Preference: If you prefer smoother meatballs, you can use a food processor to finely chop the onion and bell pepper before adding them to the meat mixture.
- Creamy Comfort: The combination of creamy sauce and well-seasoned meatballs makes this dish a comfort food classic that's both satisfying and delicious.
- Sauce Thickening: Adding flour to the pan after cooking the meatballs creates a roux, which thickens the sauce. Browning the flour slightly removes the raw taste.
- Cream and Broth: The combination of heavy cream and broth creates a rich and flavorful sauce that coats the meatballs. Adjust the ratio for your desired thickness.
- Flavorings: Mustard, ground black pepper, and salt contribute to the sauce's flavor profile. Adjust these seasonings based on your taste preferences.
- Sauce Choice: The "sauce" mentioned can vary depending on your preference. You might use tomato sauce, gravy, cream-based sauce, or another type of sauce that complements the meatballs.

- Serving: After cooking the meatballs, they are returned to the pan with the sauce to absorb the flavors. This ensures that the meatballs are coated evenly and the dish is well balanced.

- Variations: Customize the recipe with your choice of ground meat or additional spices. You can also experiment with different sauces to create unique flavor profiles.

- Garnish: Freshly chopped herbs, such as parsley or chives, can be sprinkled over the dish before serving for added color and freshness.

- Accompaniments: Serve the meatballs and sauce over pasta, rice, mashed potatoes, or with crusty bread for a complete meal.

- Taste and Adjust: Taste the sauce before serving and adjust the seasoning as needed. You can add more salt, pepper, or other seasonings to achieve the desired flavor balance.

17. Smoked Mackerel on Rye

When talking about masterpiece sandwiches, this Scandinavian-themed sandwich is on top of the list of mouthwatering sandwich delicacies!!!

Preparation Time: 10 minutes

Cook Time: nil

Serve: 1

List of Ingredients:

- 30g of flaked mackerel filets (smoked and skinless)
- 30g of Crème Fraîche
- 1 chunked apple (cored)
- 3 halved cherry tomatoes
- 1 lemon (wedged)
- 1 tbsp of horseradish sauce
- 2 slices of halved dark rye bread (pumpernickel)
- 1 tbsp of chopped dill
- 1 sliced celery stick
- 40g of beetroot (chunked)

AAAAAAAAAAAAAAAAAAAAAAA

Methods:

A. Place slices of rye bread on a plate to form the base for the dish.

B. In a bowl, mix together horseradish sauce, diced apples, chopped celery, diced tomatoes, crème fraîche, and chopped dill. This flavorful mixture will serve as a topping for the bread.

C. Spread the prepared horseradish mixture over the rye bread slices, creating a flavorful and creamy foundation.

D. Arrange smoked mackerel filets over the dill mixture on the bread. The smoked mackerel adds a rich and smoky flavor to the dish.

E. Place slices of beetroot over the smoked mackerel. The beetroot adds earthy sweetness and a vibrant color contrast.

F. To finish, garnish the dish with a squeeze of lemon juice. The lemon juice adds a bright and tangy element that balances the flavors.

Cooking Notes:

- Rye Bread: The choice of rye bread is integral to the dish. Its hearty texture and slightly nutty flavor pair well with the smoked mackerel and other toppings.
- Horseradish Sauce: Horseradish sauce adds a spicy and pungent kick to the dish. Adjust the amount to your taste preference, considering how much heat you enjoy.
- Toppings: The mixture of apples, celery, tomatoes, crème fraîche, and dill adds layers of flavor and textures. The apples provide a touch of sweetness, while celery adds crunch and dill contributes freshness.
- Smoked Mackerel: Smoked mackerel is a flavorful and oily fish that pairs well with the creamy and tangy toppings. Its smokiness adds depth to the dish.
- Beetroot: Sliced beetroot not only adds a pop of color but also complements the other flavors with its earthy sweetness. You can use cooked or pickled beetroot.
- Lemon Juice: The squeeze of lemon juice serves as a finishing touch that brightens the dish and brings out the flavors of the other ingredients.
- Presentation: The arrangement of the toppings over the bread allows for an attractive presentation. Place the fish filets neatly over the dill mixture, and then layer the beetroot slices on top.
- Balance: The combination of smoky fish, creamy toppings, and the tangy lemon juice creates a balanced and satisfying dish that's both savory and refreshing.
- Serving: Smoked Mackerel on Rye is an ideal choice for breakfast, brunch, or a light lunch. The dish is simple yet flavorful, making it a versatile option for various occasions.
- Customization: Feel free to customize the dish by adding or omitting ingredients based on your preferences. You can experiment with additional toppings like capers, red onion, or different herbs.
- Garnish: You can enhance the dish's appearance and flavor with additional garnishes such as chopped fresh dill, chives, or a sprinkle of black pepper.

- Accompaniments: This dish can be served on its own or paired with a side salad, fresh fruit, or even a creamy soup for a more substantial meal.

18. Blabarssoppa

If you want to serve it cold in Summer or hot in winter, this Swedish blueberries soup has got you covered!! It is suitable for any weather!!!

Preparation Time: 07 minutes

Cook Time: 18 minutes

Serve: 1

List of Ingredients:

- 1 tsp of water
- 1 tbsp of whipped cream
- 2 tbsp of sugar
- 1 cup of blueberries
- 1 tsp of cornstarch

AAAAAAAAAAAAAAAAAAAAAA

Methods:

A. In a bowl, mix cornstarch with water, creating a slurry. Set it aside for later use.

B. In a pan, combine sugar, blueberries, and 1 cup of water. Cook the mixture and let it simmer for approximately 10 minutes. This allows the blueberries to release their flavors and create a base for the soup.

C. Turn off the heat and allow the blueberry mixture to cool down before using an immersion blender to blend it until smooth. This step helps create a smooth and consistent texture for the soup.

D. Once blended, turn the heat back on and add the cornstarch mixture to the pan. Continuously stir the mixture until it thickens into a soup-like consistency. The cornstarch helps thicken the soup and gives it a smooth, velvety texture.

E. Once the soup has reached the desired thickness, it's ready to be served. Ladle the soup into bowls.

F. For an added touch, garnish the soup with a drizzle of cream. The cream adds richness and a delightful contrast to the fruity flavor of the soup.

Cooking Notes:

- Cornstarch Slurry: Mixing cornstarch with water creates a slurry that helps thicken the soup evenly. Make sure to stir the slurry well to ensure there are no lumps before adding it to the soup.

- Blueberry Selection: Use fresh or frozen blueberries for the soup. If using frozen blueberries, make sure to thaw them before cooking.

- Cooking the Blueberries: Cooking the blueberries with sugar and water helps break down the berries and release their juices, creating the base of the soup. The sugar adds sweetness to balance the tartness of the blueberries.

- Blending: Using an immersion blender to blend the blueberry mixture creates a smooth and consistent texture. If you don't have an immersion blender, you can carefully transfer the mixture to a regular blender to blend it and then return it to the pan.

- Thickening: The cornstarch mixture is added to thicken the soup to the desired consistency. Stirring continuously is essential to prevent lumps from forming and to achieve a silky texture.

- Serving: Blabarssoppa is typically served as a cold soup, making it a refreshing option during warmer months. However, you can also enjoy it slightly warm or at room temperature, depending on your preference.

- Cream Garnish: The cream garnish adds richness and a luxurious touch to the soup. You can drizzle the cream in a decorative pattern or simply add a dollop to the center of each bowl.

- Cultural Significance: Blabarssoppa is a traditional Swedish blueberry soup that holds cultural significance and is often enjoyed as a dessert or light summer appetizer.

- Variations: Depending on personal taste, you can adjust the level of sweetness by adding more or less sugar. You can also experiment with different types of berries or even a combination of berries for a unique flavor profile.
- Presentation: Serving the soup in attractive bowls and adding a cream garnish enhances the visual appeal of the dish.
- Customization: Consider adding a sprinkle of lemon zest or a splash of citrus juice to brighten the flavors of the soup. You can also experiment with different herbs or spices for added complexity.

19. Fish Martini

Yummy!!!

Preparation Time: 06 minutes

Cook Time: nil

Serve: 1

List of Ingredients:

- 25 ml of cranberry juice
- 20 ml of triple sec
- 1 fish candy (Swedish)
- 40 ml of vodka
- 9 ml of lemon Juice

AAAAAAAAAAAAAAAAAAAAAA

Methods:

A. Begin by filling a shaker with ice. The ice will help chill and mix the ingredients effectively.

B. Pour the specified amounts of juices, triple sec, and vodka into the shaker. These ingredients form the base of your Fish Martini and contribute to its flavor profile.

C. Shake the shaker vigorously to thoroughly mix the ingredients and chill the mixture. Shaking also adds aeration, giving the cocktail a pleasing texture.

D. Once shaken, strain the mixed liquid from the shaker into a glass. Straining helps ensure that any ice shards or fruit pulp are left behind, resulting in a smooth cocktail.

E. To enhance the presentation and tie in the fish theme, garnish the cocktail with a piece of fish candy. This playful touch adds visual interest to the cocktail.

Cooking Notes:

- Ice in the Shaker: Adding ice to the shaker helps in chilling the ingredients quickly and efficiently, creating a refreshing cocktail.

- Choice of Juices: The recipe specifies juices, triple sec, and vodka. You can choose citrus juices like orange, lemon, or lime, depending on your preference and the flavor you want to achieve.

- Triple Sec: Triple sec is an orange-flavored liqueur that adds sweetness and citrusy notes to the cocktail. It's a common ingredient in many cocktails.

- Shaking: Vigorous shaking is important to mix the ingredients thoroughly and chill the cocktail. You can use a cocktail shaker or a mixing glass with a shaker tin to shake the ingredients.

- Straining: Straining the cocktail ensures a smooth and refined texture, without ice or pulp from the fruit juices.

- Garnish: The fish candy garnish adds a playful and thematic element to the cocktail. You can find fish-shaped candies or create your own using edible materials.

- Glass Choice: Consider serving the Fish Martini in a martini glass or a glass that complements the cocktail's presentation.

- Variations: Feel free to experiment with variations. You can adjust the ratios of ingredients to suit your taste. Additionally, you can explore using flavored vodkas or different liqueurs for unique flavors.

- Presentation: The garnish and the overall presentation contribute to the visual appeal of the cocktail. A well-presented cocktail is more enjoyable to drink.

- Serving Occasion: The Fish Martini can be served as a fun and creative cocktail at themed parties, gatherings, or events. Its unique name and playful garnish make it a conversation starter.

- Drink Responsibly: As with any alcoholic beverage, it's important to enjoy the Fish Martini responsibly and in moderation.

- Creative Touch: The Fish Martini showcases how cocktails can be creative and artistic, incorporating visual elements to enhance the overall drinking experience.

20. Polar Bear Shot

Crystal clear!!!

Preparation Time: 05 minutes

Cook Time: nil

Serve: 1

List of Ingredients:

- 1 ounce of Crème de Menthe
- 1 ounce of white crème de cacao

AAAAAAAAAAAAAAAAAAAAAA

Methods:

A. Begin by pouring 1 ounce of Crème de Menthe and 1 ounce of white crème de cacao into a shaker filled with ice. These two ingredients form the basis of the Polar Bear Shot.

B. Shake the shaker vigorously to mix the ingredients and chill the mixture. Shaking also adds a frothy texture to the cocktail.

C. Once shaken, strain the mixed liquid from the shaker into a glass. Straining ensures that any ice shards or small ice crystals are left behind, resulting in a smooth shot.

D. The Polar Bear Shot is now ready to be served. Present the shot in a small glass or shot glass for a visually appealing presentation.

Cooking Notes:

- Crème de Menthe: This mint-flavored liqueur adds a refreshing and cool minty flavor to the shot.
- White Crème de Cacao: This sweet and creamy chocolate-flavored liqueur balances the minty notes with its rich and smooth taste.
- Shaker: Using a shaker with ice is essential to mix and chill the ingredients effectively. A cocktail shaker with a built-in strainer is preferable.
- Shaking Time: Shake the mixture for about 10-15 seconds to ensure thorough mixing and proper chilling.

- Straining: Straining is important to achieve a smooth and consistent texture without any ice chips. A Hawthorne strainer or a fine mesh strainer can be used for this step.

- Glass Choice: Use small shot glasses for serving the Polar Bear Shot. The presentation in a shot glass enhances the appeal of the cocktail.

- Chilled Glass: For an extra chill, you can place the shot glass in the freezer for a few minutes before pouring in the cocktail.

- Serving Occasion: The Polar Bear Shot is a playful and visually striking option for parties, gatherings, and themed events.

- Garnish: While the recipe doesn't specify a garnish, you can consider adding a small mint leaf or a sprinkle of cocoa powder on top of the shot for an extra touch.

- Temperature: The Polar Bear Shot is traditionally served chilled. The combination of cool mint and chocolate flavors makes it a refreshing choice.

- Customization: Feel free to experiment with proportions to achieve the desired balance of flavors. You can adjust the amounts of Crème de Menthe and white crème de cacao to suit your taste preferences.

- Moderation: As with any alcoholic beverage, it's important to consume shots like the Polar Bear Shot responsibly and in moderation.

- Creative Touch: The Polar Bear Shot showcases how simple ingredients can create a delightful and visually appealing cocktail. Its name and colors make it a conversation starter at events.

21. Egg Coffee

Drinking coffee in a regular way can get boring at times. Hence, this is why we are suggesting you try out this Scandinavian coffee recipe that we are sure will blow your mind!!!

Preparation Time: 05 minutes

Cook Time: 10 minutes

Serve: 1

List of Ingredients:

- 50 ml of condensed milk
- 50 ml of strong espresso
- 1 pinch of vanilla extract
- 1 egg yolk
- 2 tbsp of grated dark chocolate

AAAAAAAAAAAAAAAAAAAAA

Methods:

A. Start by mixing milk, egg yolk, and vanilla extract in a bowl until the mixture becomes foamy and pale. This mixture will serve as a creamy and flavorful addition to the coffee.

B. Place a heat proof glass inside a larger bowl filled with boiling water. This step helps warm the glass before pouring in the coffee.

C. Pour the desired amount of coffee into the preheated glass. The heated glass will help maintain the temperature of the coffee.

D. Gently spoon or pour the foamy milk, yolk, and vanilla mixture on top of the coffee as a creamy topping. This adds richness and flavor to the coffee.

E. Sprinkle a bit of grated chocolate on top of the coffee for added texture and a touch of sweetness.

F. Your Egg Coffee is now ready to enjoy. Sip and savor the unique blend of flavors and textures.

Cooking Notes:

- Milk and Egg Mixture: Whisking milk, egg yolk, and vanilla extract together creates a creamy and frothy mixture. The egg yolk adds richness and depth to the coffee's flavor.

- Vanilla Extract: Vanilla extract contributes a pleasant aroma and a hint of sweetness to the mixture. You can adjust the amount of vanilla extract to your taste.

- Heat Proof Glass: Placing the glass in boiling water helps warm it, ensuring that the coffee stays hot for longer.

- Coffee Choice: Choose your preferred type of coffee, such as espresso or strong brewed coffee, to form the base of your Egg Coffee.

- Layering: The coffee and milk mixture naturally create distinct layers, adding to the visual appeal of the drink.

- Grated Chocolate: The grated chocolate serves as a garnish, adding a touch of chocolate flavor and texture. You can use dark chocolate, milk chocolate, or white chocolate based on your preference.

- Enjoyment: Egg Coffee offers a combination of the familiar (coffee) and the unique (egg yolk and vanilla mixture). It's a comforting and indulgent beverage.

- Variations: For those who enjoy experimenting, consider adding a sprinkle of cinnamon or nutmeg on top for added warmth and flavor complexity.

- Serving Occasion: Egg Coffee can be enjoyed as a cozy morning treat or a special beverage during gatherings.

- Balancing Flavors: When creating the milk and egg mixture, ensure that the vanilla extract and sweetness are well balanced. Taste as you go to achieve the desired flavor profile.

- Cultural Significance: Egg Coffee might have cultural significance in certain regions, such as Vietnam, where it's known as "cà phê trứng." It's important to approach traditional recipes with respect and an understanding of their origins.

- Moderation: Given the inclusion of raw egg yolk, it's important to ensure that the eggs are fresh and of high quality. Some individuals may prefer to use pasteurized eggs for safety.
- Texture and Taste: The creamy milk and egg mixture adds a velvety texture and subtle sweetness to the coffee. The flavors are balanced and nuanced, creating a delightful drinking experience.

22. Sausage Stroganoff

We all can agree that sausages are not the prettiest food items to eat, but with this Scandinavian recipe, you'd Love sausage more!!!

Preparation Time: 10 minutes

Cook Time: 16 minutes

Serve: 3

List of Ingredients:

- 1 tbsp of coconut oil
- 1 chopped medium onion
- 1 chopped tomato
- 1 chopped garlic
- 1 tsp of ketchup
- 1 pinch of oregano
- 1 dash of Worcestershire sauce
- 1 pinch of salt
- 1 tsp of black pepper
- 200g of tinned tomatoes
- 60ml of stock
- 200g of Swedish sausage (cut into long strips)
- 1 tsp of butter
- 1 pinch of chili powder
- 1 pinch of paprika
- 60ml of cream

AAAAAAAAAAAAAAAAAAAAAA

Methods:

A. Start by placing butter and coconut oil in a pan, then heat them. These fats create a flavorful base for sautéing and add richness to the dish.

B. Once the fats are heated, sauté the onions in the pan. Sautéing onions releases their natural sweetness and adds a savory foundation to the Stroganoff.

C. Add minced garlic to the pan and continue cooking for about 2 minutes. Garlic enhances the overall flavor profile and adds aromatic depth to the dish.

D. Introduce the sausages to the pan and cook-fry them for approximately 4 minutes. Cooking the sausages allows them to develop their flavors and incorporate them into the dish.

E. Incorporate ketchup, sauce, diced tomatoes, salt, chili powder, ground black pepper, paprika, and oregano into the pan. These seasonings contribute a blend of flavors and spice levels to the Stroganoff.

F. Include additional canned tomatoes and stock to the pan's contents. This step adds more liquid and enhances the sauce's consistency. Allow the mixture to cook for approximately 6 minutes, allowing flavors to meld and develop.

G. Finish the dish by adding cream to the pan. The cream adds a creamy and indulgent element to the Stroganoff, creating a luscious sauce.

H. Your Sausage Stroganoff is now ready to be served. Enjoy the flavorful mixture over rice or another preferred base.

Cooking Notes:

- Butter and Coconut Oil: Using a combination of butter and coconut oil provides a rich and aromatic foundation for sautéing the ingredients.
- Onions: Sautéing onions until translucent enhances their sweetness and adds a foundational flavor to the dish.

- Garlic: Adding minced garlic contributes a savory depth to the Stroganoff. Be careful not to overcook the garlic, as it can become bitter.
- Sausages: Cooking the sausages in the pan helps develop their flavors and contributes to the overall taste of the dish.
- Seasonings: The combination of ketchup, sauce, diced tomatoes, salt, chili powder, pepper, paprika, and oregano adds a balance of flavors, from tangy to spicy and aromatic.
- Canned Tomatoes and Stock: The canned tomatoes and stock add liquid to the dish, creating a sauce that coats the ingredients and brings the flavors together.
- Cream: Adding cream at the end adds richness and creaminess to the sauce. Be sure to stir well to incorporate the cream evenly.
- Serving Suggestions: Sausage Stroganoff can be served over rice, pasta, or even mashed potatoes.
- Texture and Flavor: The dish combines tender sausages, flavorful sauce, and aromatic spices, resulting in a hearty and satisfying meal.
- Customization: Feel free to adjust the spices and seasonings to your taste preferences. You can also add vegetables like bell peppers or mushrooms for added texture and nutrition.
- Balanced Meal: Sausage Stroganoff offers a balanced combination of protein, carbohydrates, and fats, making it a complete and filling dish.
- Culinary Heritage: Stroganoff is a classic dish with variations across different cuisines. The sausage adaptation adds its own unique twist to the traditional recipe.
- Cooking Skill: This recipe involves sautéing, simmering, and combining flavors. It's suitable for home cooks looking to create a flavorful and comforting meal.

23. Rice Pudding

This comfort meal is one extraordinary dessert that is nourishing and appetizing!!!

Preparation Time: 10 minutes

Cook Time: 30 minutes

Serve: 2

List of Ingredients:

- 2 cups of milk
- 4 tbsp of cream
- 1 pinch of ground cardamom
- 3 handfuls of Arborio rice
- 1 cup of cranberry sauce
- 1 tbsp of vanilla bean seeds
- 4 tbsp of granulated sugar

AAAAAAAAAAAAAAAAAAAAAA

Methods:

A. In a pot, combine cream, vanilla seeds, milk, sugar, rice, and cardamom. This mixture forms the base of your rice pudding.

B. Simmer the mixture over low heat for about 30 minutes. The goal is to cook the rice until it becomes soft and the mixture thickens.

C. After the cooking time, your rice pudding should have reached a creamy and satisfying consistency.

D. Your rice pudding is now ready to be served. To add a burst of flavor and sweetness, serve it with a side of cranberry sauce.

Cooking Notes:

- Cream and Milk: The combination of cream and milk contributes to the creaminess and richness of the rice pudding.

- Vanilla Seeds: The use of vanilla seeds adds a delightful aromatic flavor to the pudding.

- Sugar: Sugar adds sweetness to the dish. Adjust the amount of sugar to your taste preferences.

- Rice: Use short-grain rice for rice pudding, as it releases starch during cooking and creates a creamy texture.

- Cardamom: Cardamom adds a warm and fragrant element to the dish. Make sure not to overpower the dish with too much cardamom.

- Simmering: Simmer the mixture over low heat to avoid scorching and to allow the rice to cook evenly.

- Texture: The rice should be soft and tender, and the pudding should have a creamy consistency. If the pudding becomes too thick, you can adjust the consistency by adding more milk.

- Cranberry Sauce: Serving the rice pudding with cranberry sauce complements the creamy sweetness with a tart and fruity note.

- Presentation: You can serve the rice pudding in individual bowls or a larger dish. Drizzle the cranberry sauce over the pudding just before serving.

- Customization: Feel free to customize the recipe by adding other toppings, such as chopped nuts, cinnamon, or a sprinkle of nutmeg.

- Serving Occasions: Rice pudding is a comforting and versatile dessert that can be enjoyed as a cozy treat or a satisfying conclusion to a meal.

- Culinary Heritage: Rice pudding is a classic dessert enjoyed in various forms across different cultures. It's interesting to explore the different variations and flavor profiles.

- Texture and Flavor: A well-prepared rice pudding should be creamy, with tender rice grains and a balance of sweetness and warmth from the vanilla and cardamom.
- Nostalgia: Rice pudding often evokes feelings of nostalgia and comfort, making it a favorite among many.
- Balancing Flavors: The creamy rice pudding pairs beautifully with the tangy and sweet cranberry sauce. The contrast in flavors adds depth to the dish.
- Cultural Significance: Rice pudding may hold cultural significance in various regions, and different variations might include local ingredients and traditions.
- Enjoyment: The satisfaction of a well-made rice pudding lies in its comforting creaminess and the interplay of flavors. The cranberry sauce adds a burst of brightness to each bite.

24. Skagen Prawn Salad

Want to serve prawns as an appetizer or even as a meal? Don't underestimate the power of this delicious Scandinavian Prawn recipe!! It is mind-blowing!!!

Preparation Time: 07 minutes

Cook Time: nil

Serve: 2

List of Ingredients:

- 1 tbsp of chopped parsley
- 130g of cooked Atlantic prawns (peeled)
- 1 tsp of lemon Juice
- 1 dash of pepper
- 1 tbsp of sour cream
- 1 tbsp of coconut oil
- 1 tsp of lemon zest
- 1 handful of chopped onion (red)
- 1 pinch of salt

AAAAAAAAAAAAAAAAAAAAAA

Methods:

A. In a large bowl, combine the freshly ground pepper, lemon juice, sour cream, oil, lemon zest, and a pinch of salt. These ingredients form the flavorful base of the Skagen prawn salad.

B. Add the peeled and cooked prawns to the bowl. These prawns will add a delicate seafood flavor and a satisfying texture to the salad.

C. Finely chop the onion and fresh parsley. Incorporate both the onion and parsley into the bowl, adding a layer of crunch and herbaceous freshness to the salad.

D. Toss all the ingredients in the bowl together. Make sure the dressing and ingredients are evenly distributed, ensuring that every bite is full of flavor and texture.

E. Your Skagen prawn salad is now ready to be enjoyed. Serve it as an appetizer, light meal, or a refreshing side dish.

Cooking Notes:

- Pepper: Freshly ground black pepper adds a touch of heat and complexity to the salad's flavor profile.

- Lemon Juice and Zest: Lemon juice and zest contribute zesty and tangy notes that complement the seafood and other ingredients.

- Sour Cream: Sour cream provides creaminess and tanginess to the dressing, enhancing the overall mouthfeel and flavor.

- Oil: A good-quality oil, such as olive oil, adds a smooth texture to the dressing and helps bind the flavors together.

- Salt: A pinch of salt enhances the overall taste and balances the flavors.

- Prawns: Use cooked and peeled prawns for convenience. Their sweet and briny flavor is a highlight of the salad.

- Serving Vessels: Consider serving the Skagen prawn salad in small bowls or on individual plates for an elegant presentation. Alternatively, you can serve it in lettuce cups for a light and refreshing twist.

- Make-Ahead: You can prepare the dressing and chop the onion and parsley ahead of time. Keep them refrigerated until you're ready to assemble the salad to save time.

- Seafood Variations: While prawns are traditional, you can explore other seafood options such as crab, lobster, or even smoked salmon to create your own seafood salad variation.

- Cream Alternatives: If you're looking for a lighter option, you can substitute Greek yogurt or a combination of yogurt and mayonnaise for the sour cream.

- Lemon Balance: Adjust the amount of lemon juice and zest based on your preference for tartness. Taste as you go to achieve the right balance of flavors.

- Prawn Presentation: To enhance the visual appeal, consider reserving a few whole prawns to arrange on top of the salad before serving.

- Bread Choices: Apart from crispbread, you can serve Skagen prawn salad on toasted baguette slices, crostini, or even small lettuce leaves for a low-carb option.

- Avocado Addition: For an extra creamy element, you can add diced avocado to the salad. It pairs well with the seafood and adds a buttery texture.

- Chill Before Serving: Allow the salad to chill in the refrigerator for about 30 minutes before serving. This helps the flavors to meld and the salad to be refreshingly cool.

- Dill Infusion: If you enjoy the flavor of dill, consider adding chopped fresh dill to the salad. It's a classic herb that pairs exceptionally well with seafood.

- Wine Pairing: Skagen prawn salad goes beautifully with a crisp white wine, such as a Sauvignon Blanc or a Chardonnay, enhancing the seafood flavors.

- Local Ingredients: When making traditional dishes like Skagen prawn salad, using locally sourced and seasonal ingredients can further enhance the dish's flavors.

- Travel Through Food: Exploring international recipes like this one allows you to virtually travel and experience different cultures through their cuisine.

- Portion Control: Consider the size of the prawns and the amount of salad served per person. It's important to strike a balance between the prawns and the other ingredients.

- Sustainability: When purchasing seafood, opt for sustainable and responsibly sourced options to support eco-friendly practices.

- Elevating Leftovers: If you have leftover Skagen prawn salad, you can use it as a filling for sushi rolls or mix it with cooked pasta for a flavorful pasta salad.

- Aromatic Herbs: If you want to experiment with additional herbs, consider adding a touch of tarragon, chives, or even mint for a unique twist.

- Texture Harmony: The combination of the creamy dressing, the succulent prawns, and the fresh herbs creates a delightful contrast in textures.

- Pairing with Greens: To make the dish even more substantial, you can serve the Skagen prawn salad on a bed of mixed greens or arugula.

- Homemade Crispbread: If you're feeling adventurous, you can try making your own crispbread to serve alongside the salad for an authentic Scandinavian experience.
- Serving Season: Skagen prawn salad is particularly popular during the summer months due to its light and refreshing nature. It's a great addition to picnics and outdoor gatherings.
- Onion: Finely chopped onion adds a mild sharpness and crunch to the salad.
- Parsley: Fresh parsley contributes a burst of color and herbaceous freshness. Flat-leaf parsley is commonly used for its milder flavor.
- Tossing: Tossing the ingredients together ensures that the dressing coats all the components and that the flavors meld harmoniously.
- Presentation: Serve the Skagen prawn salad on individual plates or as a shared dish. Garnish with additional parsley leaves for an attractive presentation.
- Crispbread: Crispbread, a type of Scandinavian cracker, is a classic accompaniment to Skagen prawn salad. Its crisp texture complements the creamy salad.
- Variations: Skagen prawn salad can be customized to your preferences. Some variations include adding dill, red onion, or even a touch of horseradish for extra zing.
- Cultural Context: Skagen prawn salad is a classic Scandinavian dish, named after the Skagen peninsula in Denmark. It showcases the region's seafood and culinary heritage.
- Texture and Flavor Harmony: The salad combines creamy, tangy, and fresh elements, with the prawns providing a satisfying bite.
- Nutritional Value: Skagen prawn salad offers protein from the prawns, healthy fats from the oil, and freshness from the herbs.
- Versatility: Skagen prawn salad can be enjoyed on its own, as a topping for bread, or even as a filling for sandwiches or wraps.
- Enjoyment: The combination of fresh seafood, creamy dressing, and aromatic herbs makes Skagen prawn salad a delightful and appetizing dish.

25. Remoulade

Let's try to cook remoulade the Scandinavian way!!!

Preparation Time: 10 minutes

Cook Time: nil

Serve: 6

List of Ingredients:

- 2 tbsp of chopped cabbage
- 6 tbsp of mayonnaise
- 2 tbsp of chopped gherkins
- 2 tbsp of chopped chives
- 1 tbsp of sugar
- 1 pinch of pepper
- 2 tbsp of sour cream
- 2 tbsp of chopped carrots
- 2 tbsp of lemon juice
- 2 tbsp of mustard
- 2 tbsp of chopped red onion
- 2 tbsp of turmeric
- 1 tbsp of salt

AAAAAAAAAAAAAAAAAAAAAA

Methods:

A. In a mixing bowl, combine the chopped cabbage, mayonnaise, chopped gherkins, chopped chives, sugar, a pinch of pepper, sour cream, chopped carrots, lemon juice, mustard, chopped red onion, turmeric, and salt. These ingredients will form the flavorful base of the remoulade sauce.

B. Mix all the ingredients well to ensure that the flavors are evenly distributed throughout the sauce. The combination of textures and flavors from the vegetables and condiments will create a balanced and tasty sauce.

C. After mixing, cover the bowl and let the remoulade chill in the refrigerator for about 40 minutes. Chilling allows the flavors to meld and develop, resulting in a more harmonious and delicious sauce.

Cooking Notes:

- Chopped Cabbage: The cabbage provides a fresh crunch and texture to the remoulade. It's important to finely chop the cabbage so that it blends well with the other ingredients.
- Mayonnaise: Mayonnaise forms the creamy base of the remoulade and contributes to its rich texture.
- Chopped Gherkins: Gherkins (pickles) add a tangy and slightly sour flavor to the sauce. Chop them finely for even distribution.
- Chopped Chives: Chives offer a mild onion-like flavor and a touch of color. They should be finely chopped.
- Sugar: A small amount of sugar balances the flavors and reduces any sharpness.
- Pepper: A pinch of pepper adds a subtle warmth to the sauce.
- Sour Cream: Sour cream enhances the creaminess and tanginess of the remoulade.
- Chopped Carrots: Finely chopped carrots contribute sweetness and color to the sauce.

- Lemon Juice: Lemon juice provides acidity and freshness. Adjust the amount to taste.
- Mustard: Mustard adds a zesty and tangy note to the remoulade.
- Chopped Red Onion: Red onion imparts a milder onion flavor and color contrast to the sauce.
- Turmeric: Turmeric not only adds a hint of color but also offers its health benefits and earthy flavor.
- Salt: Salt enhances the overall taste of the sauce.
- Mixing: Thoroughly mixing the ingredients ensures that each bite of remoulade is well-balanced in terms of flavor and texture.
- Chilling: Allowing the remoulade to chill in the refrigerator allows the flavors to meld and intensify.
- Serving: Serve the chilled remoulade as a versatile and flavorful accompaniment to a variety of dishes.
- Versatility: Remoulade is a classic sauce that compliments seafood, meats, sandwiches, and more. It adds a burst of flavor to various dishes.
- Culinary Heritage: Remoulade sauce has its roots in French cuisine but has variations in different culinary traditions.
- Customization: Feel free to adjust the quantities of the ingredients to suit your taste preferences. You can also add other herbs or spices for a personalized touch.
- Enjoyment: The combination of creamy, tangy, and crunchy elements makes remoulade a delightful condiment that enhances the overall dining experience.

26. Jansson's Temptation

On cold nights, this delicacy is not just Jansson's Temptation. It is our joint Temptation!!

Preparation Time: 20 minutes

Cook Time: 30 minutes

Serve: 3

List of Ingredients:

- 3 peeled potatoes (cut into strips)
- 1 tsp of melted butter
- 6 Swedish anchovy filets
- 1 medium onion (cut into strips)
- 1 tbsp of dry breadcrumbs
- 10 tbsp of heavy cream

AAAAAAAAAAAAAAAAAAAAAAAA

Methods:

A. Begin by preheating your oven to 422 degrees F (215 degrees C). Preheating ensures that the oven reaches the desired temperature before you start baking.

B. Take a buttered baking dish and spread a layer of thinly sliced onions at the base. The onions will provide a flavorful foundation for the dish.

C. Arrange the anchovy filets on top of the onions. Anchovies add a salty and umami-rich element to the dish.

D. Now, layer the sliced potatoes over the anchovies. The potatoes will form the main body of the dish and provide substance.

E. Pour heavy cream over the layered ingredients. The cream adds richness and moisture to the dish as it bakes.

F. In a separate bowl, combine softened butter and breadcrumbs. This mixture will form a crunchy and golden topping for the Jansson's Temptation.

G. Spread the buttery breadcrumb mixture evenly over the layer of sliced potatoes and cream.

H. Place the baking dish in the preheated oven and bake until the potatoes are cooked through and the breadcrumb topping turns golden brown. This baking process allows all the flavors to meld together while creating a delightful contrast in textures.

I. Once the dish is fully cooked and the top is golden, remove it from the oven.

J. Serve the Jansson's Temptation while it's still warm. The dish is best enjoyed fresh from the oven, when the flavors are at their peak.

Cooking Notes:

- Onions: Slicing the onions thinly ensures that they cook evenly and blend well with the other ingredients.

- Anchovies: Anchovies are a traditional ingredient in Jansson's Temptation, providing a distinct umami flavor. You can adjust the amount based on your preference.

- Potato Consistency: While slicing the potatoes, aim for uniform thickness to ensure even cooking. Thicker slices might need slightly more baking time.

- Potato Parboiling: If you're looking for an even softer and creamier texture for the potatoes, consider parboiling them for a few minutes before layering.

- Cream Distribution: When pouring the heavy cream over the layered ingredients, ensure it's distributed evenly to prevent any dry spots during baking.

- Anchovy Alternatives: If you're not a fan of anchovies, you can consider substituting them with smoked herring or even sautéed mushrooms for an earthy flavor.

- Breadcrumb Flavor: Enhance the flavor of the breadcrumb topping by adding a pinch of freshly grated nutmeg or a sprinkle of chopped fresh herbs, such as parsley.

- Portion Sizes: Consider the portion sizes when arranging the ingredients. Adjust the size of the baking dish and the quantities of each ingredient accordingly.

- Cream Variation: For a lighter version, you can use a combination of milk and light cream instead of heavy cream. This will reduce the richness while maintaining the creamy texture.

- Gluten-Free Option: If you're following a gluten-free diet, use gluten-free breadcrumbs or crushed gluten-free crackers for the topping.

- Serving Side Dishes: Jansson's Temptation pairs well with simple sides like a crisp green salad or steamed vegetables to balance out the richness.

- Traditional Accompaniments: In Sweden, Jansson's Temptation is often served with pickled beets or a tangy lingonberry sauce for a contrast in flavors.

- Layering Precision: To ensure each layer is evenly distributed, consider alternating layers of onions, anchovies, and potatoes. This provides a consistent flavor profile.

- Texture Contrast: The creamy interior of the dish paired with the crunchy breadcrumb topping offers a delightful textural contrast that's enjoyable to eat.

- Storage: Leftover Jansson's Temptation can be stored in the refrigerator. Reheat individual portions in the oven to maintain the crispiness of the topping.

- Recipe Scaling: This recipe is easily scalable for larger gatherings. Just adjust the quantities of the ingredients accordingly.

- Cooking Time Observation: Keep an eye on the dish as it bakes. If the breadcrumb topping starts to brown too quickly, you can tent it with aluminum foil to prevent over-browning.

- Baking Position: Placing the baking dish on the middle rack of the oven ensures even cooking and browning of the dish.

- Cultural Exploration: Trying traditional dishes like Jansson's Temptation provides an opportunity to immerse yourself in the culinary heritage of different cultures.

- Cheese Addition: If you enjoy cheese, you can sprinkle grated cheese over the layers for added richness and flavor.

- Garnish Idea: Before serving, consider garnishing the dish with a sprinkle of chopped fresh chives or parsley for a burst of color and freshness.

- Visual Appeal: The golden-brown topping of the dish can be quite visually appealing. Use this as an opportunity to present the dish beautifully on the dining table.

- Taste Layering: Think about the layering of flavors as you arrange the ingredients. The saltiness of the anchovies and the sweetness of the onions should harmonize with the creamy potatoes and the buttery breadcrumb topping.

- Potatoes: Use starchy potatoes like Russet potatoes for this dish. They hold their shape well and create a creamy texture as they bake.

- Heavy Cream: The cream adds richness and creaminess to the dish. You can use full-fat cream for the best results.

- Butter and Breadcrumbs: Combining butter and breadcrumbs creates a crispy and golden topping, adding texture and flavor to the dish.

- Baking Time: The baking time can vary based on your oven and the thickness of the potato slices. Check for doneness by inserting a fork into the potatoes; they should be tender.

- Serving: Jansson's Temptation is often served as a main course or as a side dish with traditional Swedish meals.

- Tradition: This dish has its roots in Swedish cuisine and is often enjoyed during holidays and celebrations.

- Variations: Some variations of Jansson's Temptation include adding creamed spinach or grated cheese to the layers.

- Enjoyment: The combination of creamy potatoes, savory anchovies, and a crispy breadcrumb topping makes Jansson's Temptation a comforting and flavorful dish.

27. Swedish 75

Get your dinner date started with this delicious classic cocktail!!

Preparation Time: 05 minutes

Cook Time: nil

Serve: 1

List of Ingredients:

- 4 tbsp of dry sparkling wine
- 1 tbsp of lingonberry jam
- 3 tbsp of gin
- 1 tbsp of lemon juice

AAAAAAAAAAAAAAAAAAAAAAA

Methods:

A. In a glass filled with ice, combine the lingonberry jam, gin, and lemon juice. Mixing the ingredients in a glass with ice helps to chill and dilute the flavors.

B. Stir the mixture well to ensure that the jam is fully incorporated with the gin and lemon juice. This step ensures a balanced and cohesive flavor profile.

C. Top off the mixture with sparkling wine. The addition of sparkling wine adds effervescence and a celebratory touch to the cocktail.

D. Garnish the Swedish 75 cocktail with a few lingonberries. Lingonberries are a traditional Swedish berry that adds a pop of color and a hint of tartness to the drink.

E. Enjoy your Swedish 75 cocktail! Sip and savor the harmonious blend of flavors, including the fruity sweetness of the jam, the botanical notes of the gin, the citrusy zing of the lemon juice, and the lively bubbles of the sparkling wine.

Cooking Notes:

- Lingonberry Jam: Lingonberry jam is a common ingredient in Swedish cuisine, known for its sweet-tart flavor. If you don't have lingonberry jam, you can use other fruit preserves, but lingonberry jam provides an authentic taste.

- Gin: Choose a good-quality gin for the cocktail, as it contributes to the overall flavor. The botanical and herbal notes of gin complement the fruity components.

- Lemon Juice: Freshly squeezed lemon juice adds brightness and acidity to the cocktail. Adjust the amount of lemon juice based on your personal preference.

- Sparkling Wine: You can use a dry sparkling wine, such as Champagne or Prosecco, for the cocktail. The bubbles elevate the drink and add a festive touch.

- Glass and Ice: Using a glass filled with ice helps to keep the cocktail cold and refreshing. It also dilutes the mixture slightly, balancing the flavors.

- Stirring: Stirring the cocktail is important to ensure that all the ingredients are well combined and the flavors meld together.

- Garnish: Lingonberries not only add visual appeal but also contribute a touch of natural sweetness and tartness to the drink.

- Variation: If you prefer a sweeter cocktail, you can adjust the amount of lingonberry jam or add a touch of simple syrup.

- Serving: The Swedish 75 is a delightful cocktail option for various occasions, from casual gatherings to more formal celebrations.

- Enjoyment: The Swedish 75 cocktail offers a playful twist on the classic French 75 cocktail by incorporating lingonberry jam, creating a unique and enjoyable flavor experience.

28. Sweet Potato and Rye Salad

Either served Cold or warm, this meal brings together different flavors to create a distinguishing delicious salad! This Salad is one of a kind!!

Preparation Time: 08 minutes

Cook Time: 20 minutes

Serve: 2

List of Ingredients:

- 1 tbsp of pepper
- 1 tbsp of salt
- 3 sweet potatoes (chunked and peeled)
- 1 tsp of balsamic vinegar
- 1 handful of tarragon leaves
- 100g of Feta cheese (crumbled)
- 70g of dry rye grains (cooked)
- 2 tbsp of canola oil
- 1 handful of sliced spring onions

AAAAAAAAAAAAAAAAAAAAAAA

Methods:

A. Preheat your oven to 321°F (160°C). Proper preheating ensures that your oven is at the right temperature for roasting the sweet potatoes.

B. In a mixing bowl, combine the diced sweet potatoes with a dash of pepper, a pinch of salt, and a drizzle of oil. This seasoning adds flavor and helps the sweet potatoes caramelize during roasting.

C. Spread the seasoned sweet potatoes on a baking sheet in an even layer. Roast them in the preheated oven for about 15 minutes, or until they become tender and slightly crispy on the outside.

D. While the sweet potatoes are roasting, prepare the rest of the salad. In a separate bowl, combine tarragon leaves and cheese. The tarragon brings a fresh herbal note, while the cheese adds creaminess and depth of flavor.

E. Once the sweet potatoes are cooked, add them to the tarragon and cheese mixture in the bowl. This step ensures that the warm sweet potatoes absorb the flavors of the tarragon and cheese.

F. Add cooked rye to the bowl. The rye adds a hearty and nutty element to the salad, complementing the sweet potatoes.

G. Toss the ingredients in the bowl to distribute the flavors evenly. At this point, you can adjust the seasoning with more pepper and salt, if needed.

H. Add sliced spring onions to the mixture. Spring onions provide a mild onion flavor and a pop of color.

I. Drizzle a bit more oil and vinegar over the salad. The oil adds richness, and the vinegar balances the flavors with acidity.

J. Toss the salad once more to coat all the ingredients with the oil and vinegar.

K. Serve your Sweet Potato and Rye Salad as a wholesome and flavorful dish that combines the sweetness of roasted sweet potatoes with the earthy notes of rye and the freshness of tarragon and spring onions.

Cooking Notes:

- Sweet Potatoes: Choose firm and fresh sweet potatoes with vibrant orange flesh for the best flavor and texture.

- Seasoning: The combination of pepper, salt, and oil enhances the taste and texture of the sweet potatoes during roasting.

- Roasting: Keep an eye on the sweet potatoes while roasting to prevent overcooking or burning. They should be tender on the inside and slightly crispy on the outside.

- Tarragon: Tarragon is a fragrant herb that adds a unique herbal flavor to the salad. If you're not a fan of tarragon, you can use other fresh herbs like parsley or dill.

- Cheese: Consider using a cheese that complements the other flavors, such as feta, goat cheese, or a mild blue cheese.

- Rye: Cooked rye provides a chewy and nutty texture that pairs well with the sweet potatoes.
- Spring Onions: Spring onions add a mild onion flavor and a touch of color. You can adjust the amount based on your preference.
- Oil and Vinegar: The oil adds richness, and the vinegar adds a tangy element that balances the sweetness of the sweet potatoes.
- Variations: Feel free to add other ingredients like toasted nuts, seeds, or dried fruits for added texture and flavor.
- Serving: This salad can be served as a side dish or a light main course. It's great for lunches, picnics, and gatherings.
- Enjoyment: The combination of sweet, savory, and herbal flavors, along with the contrast of textures, makes this Sweet Potato and Rye Salad a satisfying and delightful dish to enjoy.

29. Hot Toddy for a Cold

Soothing relief for a cold night!!!

Preparation Time: 06 minutes

Cook Time: 07 minutes

Serve: 1

List of Ingredients:

- 1 slice of fresh ginger
- 1 tsp of honey
- 1 dash of lemon juice
- 7 ounces of water
- 1 lemon (wedges)
- 2 cough drops (menthol)
- 2 ounces of fireball whiskey

AAAAAAAAAAAAAAAAAAAAAAA

Methods:

A. Begin by boiling the water. This will be the base of your hot toddy.

B. In a mug, combine the honey, whiskey, ginger, and cough drops. These ingredients will add flavor and soothing properties to the drink.

C. Pour the boiled water into the mug. The hot water will help dissolve the other ingredients and create a warm beverage.

D. Stir the mixture well, ensuring that the cough drops are fully dissolved. This will help release their soothing qualities into the drink.

E. Squeeze in the lemon juice. Lemon not only adds a tangy flavor but also provides a dose of vitamin C, which can be beneficial when you have a cold.

F. To garnish, add a lemon wedge to the mug. This adds a visually appealing touch to the drink and can also release some additional citrus aroma.

Cooking Notes:

- Water Temperature: Boil the water until it's hot, but not boiling vigorously. Extremely hot water can scorch the flavors of the ingredients.

- Honey: Honey is known for its soothing properties and can help relieve sore throats. It also adds a touch of sweetness to the drink.

- Whiskey: The alcohol in whiskey can provide warmth and comfort. It's important to use it in moderation and consider your personal preferences and health considerations.

- Ginger: Ginger is often used for its potential anti-inflammatory and immune-boosting properties. It also adds a spicy, comforting kick to the hot toddy.

- Cough Drops: The cough drops not only add flavor but also offer potential relief for a sore throat. Make sure they are completely dissolved before consuming.

- Lemon Juice: Lemon juice adds a refreshing tang and provides vitamin C, which can be helpful during colds and flu.

- Garnish: The lemon wedge garnish is optional but adds a nice touch to the presentation of the drink.

- Customization: You can adjust the proportions of the ingredients to suit your taste preferences. Some people prefer a stronger whiskey flavor, while others may prefer a milder taste.

- Serving: Enjoy the hot toddy while it's warm. It can be particularly comforting before bed or during a chilly day.

- Variations: Feel free to experiment with variations by adding herbs, spices, or other ingredients that you find soothing or enjoyable.

- Note: While a hot toddy can offer temporary relief from cold symptoms, it's important to stay hydrated and seek medical advice if your symptoms persist or worsen.

30. Knackebrot

These Swedish crackers are too good to be true!!

Preparation Time: 10 minutes

Cook Time: 45 minutes

Serve: 3

List of Ingredients:

- 70g of sunflower seeds
- 150g of rolled oats
- 15g of pumpkin seeds
- 25g of flaxseed
- 250ml of water
- 1 tbsp of salt
- 150g of wholemeal flour
- 30g of sesame seeds
- 1 tsp of olive oil

AAAAAAAAAAAAAAAAAAAAAA

Methods:

A. Preheat Oven: Begin by preheating the oven to 352 degrees F (180°C). This will ensure that the oven is at the right temperature when you're ready to bake the Knäckebröd.

B. Combine Ingredients: In a bowl, combine the sunflower seeds, rolled oats, pumpkin seeds, flaxseed, wholemeal flour, sesame seeds, and salt. Mix these dry ingredients together to create the base of the Knäckebröd. Add the olive oil and water to the mixture, combining everything thoroughly.

C. Prepare Baking Tray: Grease a baking tray to prevent the Knäckebröd from sticking. This will also help achieve a crisp texture during baking.

D. Spread Mixture: Pour the mixture onto the greased baking tray and spread it out to create a thin and even layer. You can use a spatula or the back of a spoon to achieve this.

E. Initial Baking: Place the tray in the preheated oven and bake for 10 minutes. This initial baking will help set the mixture and start the process of creating the crispy texture of the Knäckebröd.

F. Cut into Crackers: After the initial 10 minutes of baking, remove the tray from the oven. Use a knife or pizza cutter to carefully cut the partially baked mixture into cracker-sized pieces. This will make it easier to break the Knäckebröd into individual crackers after they're fully baked.

G. Final Baking: Place the tray with the cut mixture back into the oven. Continue baking for another 30 minutes or until the Knäckebröd turns crispy and golden brown. The extended baking time will help achieve the desired crunchiness.

H. Cool and Store: Once the Knäckebröd is baked to perfection, remove the tray from the oven and allow the crackers to cool completely. Once cooled, you can store them in an airtight container to maintain their crispness.

Cooking Notes:

- Customization: Feel free to customize the seeds and grains in the recipe according to your preference. You can experiment with different combinations to create your own unique Knäckebröd.

- Uniform Thickness: When spreading the mixture on the baking tray, aim for an even thickness throughout. This ensures that the crackers bake uniformly and achieve consistent crunchiness.

- Seed Toasting: To enhance the nutty flavors, consider toasting the sunflower seeds, pumpkin seeds, and sesame seeds in a dry pan before adding them to the mixture.

- Dough Resting: Letting the mixture sit for a few minutes after combining the wet and dry ingredients can help the seeds and oats absorb the moisture, leading to a more cohesive mixture.

- Baking Time Variability: Oven temperatures can vary, so keep an eye on the Knäckebröd during the final baking phase. You might need to adjust the baking time slightly based on your oven's behavior.

- Cracker Shapes: While squares or rectangles are the most common cracker shapes, you can use cookie cutters to create fun and unique shapes that add visual appeal.

- Nutritional Boost: Add a handful of chopped nuts, such as almonds or walnuts, to the mixture for added nutrition and texture.

- Silpat Liner: Consider using a silicone baking mat (Silpat) on the tray to prevent sticking and ensure easy removal of the crackers after baking.

- Portion Control: If you're aiming for consistent cracker sizes, use a ruler or a template to guide your cutting process after the initial baking.

- Texture Testing: To check for the desired level of crispiness, remove a cracker from the oven, let it cool, and test its texture before deciding if additional baking time is needed.

- Dietary Restrictions: Knäckebröd can easily be adapted to suit various dietary needs by using gluten-free flour or adjusting the ingredient ratios.

- Breakage Prevention: Handle the Knäckebröd gently when transferring it from the baking tray to the cooling rack. These crackers are delicate and can break if not handled with care.

- Gift Idea: Package these homemade Knäckebröd in decorative bags or jars for a thoughtful and unique gift for friends and family.

- Crisping Before Serving: If the Knäckebröd loses their crispness over time, you can place them back in a preheated oven for a short time (3-5 minutes) to re-crisp them before serving.

- Recipe Doubling: If you're making a larger batch, ensure you have enough baking trays and oven space to accommodate the doubled recipe.

- Taste Testing: As you experiment with different ingredients and variations, involve family and friends in taste testing to gather feedback and refine your recipe.

- Labeling and Dating: If you plan to store the Knäckebröd for an extended period, label the container with the baking date to ensure you consume them while they're at their best.

- Cost-Effective: Making your own Knäckebröd can be more cost-effective than store-bought versions, especially if you buy seeds and grains in bulk.

- Baking Conversion: Keep in mind that oven temperatures might need to be adjusted if your oven uses Celsius instead of Fahrenheit. Use a temperature conversion chart if necessary.

- Thickness: The thickness of the mixture spread on the baking tray will affect the final texture of the Knäckebröd. Thinner layers will result in crisper crackers.

- Flavor Variations: You can add various seasonings such as herbs, spices, or even cheese to enhance the flavor of your Knäckebröd.

- Serving: Knäckebröd is a versatile snack that can be enjoyed on its own or paired with various toppings such as cheese, spreads, or dips.

- Storage: To maintain the crispiness, store the Knäckebröd in an airtight container. If they lose their crispiness, you can re-crisp them in the oven for a short time before serving.

See You Again

Thank you for purchasing and reading my book. Your support means a lot, and I'm grateful you chose my book among many options. I write to help people like you, who appreciate every word.

Please share your thoughts on the book, as reader feedback helps me grow and improve. Your insights may even inspire others. Thanks again!

Printed in Great Britain
by Amazon

36914827R00071